simplify

simplify

a guide to caring for the soul

CAROLYN J. RASMUS

DESERET
BOOK

Salt Lake City, Utah

Library of Congress Cataloging-in-Publication Data

Rasmus, Carolyn J.
  Simplify : a guide to caring for the soul / Carolyn J. Rasmus.
      p. cm.
  Includes index.
  ISBN-13: 978-1-59038-623-1 (hardback : alk. paper)
  1. Spiritual life—The Church of Jesus Christ of Latter-day Saints.
2. Simplicity—Religious aspects—The Church of Jesus Christ of Latter-day
Saints. 3. Christian life—Mormon authors. I. Title.
  BX8656.R375 2007
  248.4—dc22   2006036440

Printed in the United States of America
Publishers Printing, Salt Lake City, UT

10   9   8   7   6   5   4   3   2   1

To Kathy
who exemplifies simplicity

contents

thank-yous

An author might pen the words for a book, but the final product is the result of the encouragement and expertise of many. I am grateful to friends who bolstered, sustained, and encouraged. Special thanks to Sheri Dew for her suggestions, support, and belief in me. Jana Erickson could not have been more helpful; what a delight to work with a product director who becomes a friend in the process.

So often unmentioned are those who work behind the scenes but are responsible for making the book editorially correct and visually appealing. Thanks to Sheryl Dickert Smith for the design and layout, Laurie Cook for typesetting, and Suzanne Brady for her superb job of editing. What a blessing to work with a team of talented and dedicated professionals.

Care for . . . the life of the soul.

—Doctrine and Covenants 101:37

Much too often I find myself running here and there, sensing I'm out of control, being busy but feeling as if I never get everything done. Unfortunately, this is not a one-time experience.

Not long ago, I came across a journal entry I wrote nearly ten years ago. "This last month has been especially hectic. I've felt overwhelmed, overcommitted, unprepared, anxious, and discouraged. I was at my highest level of 'internal churning.' The more I rushed around trying to get things done, the more frantic I felt. I could not concentrate or think clearly. I couldn't focus my thoughts. I couldn't feel the Spirit; I began to doubt my abilities—what if I have to muddle through like this for the rest of my life?"

As I talk with others, I realize I am not alone. Many in our day feel overworked, overprogrammed, overwhelmed, and out of control. We live in a fast-paced and increasingly complex world. Few of us nowadays are isolated in rural areas where family and work are our primary focus. The pressures we face daily are tremendous; they are increasing and constant. In addition to our personal and family lives, which often cause us to feel overwhelmed, television and news received instantly via cell phone or the Internet bring into our lives a multitude of circumstances—global events of monumental proportion, community concerns, and vexing world problems. Although these are external conditions over which we have little or no control, they all take a toll. As a result we feel increased stress in our lives.

> THE ADVERSARY WOULD KEEP US BUSILY ENGAGED IN A MULTITUDE OF TRIVIAL THINGS IN AN EFFORT TO KEEP US DISTRACTED FROM THE FEW VITAL THINGS THAT MAKE ALL THE DIFFERENCE.
>
> *Ardeth G. Kapp*

Stress can be a good thing. It is the stress and tension on the string of a kite that keeps it sailing in the air. The adrenaline produced by stressful conditions is critical if we are being chased by a bear or need to exert extra energy to finish a project. But the stress most people complain about comes when we feel "pushed to the edge"—out of control; when we find ourselves reacting to situations or people instead of responding in the way we would like; when simple situations or encounters with others become blown out of proportion.

When our stress levels become high, we are unable to see things in their proper perspective, solve problems creatively, communicate effectively with others, and enjoy simple pleasures. We are unable to feel at peace with ourselves and with others. Uncontrolled stress can ruin relationships, cause health problems, and make relatively easy tasks seem difficult.

I have come to believe that the most destructive aspect of stress is what it does to us spiritually. *Stress drives away the Spirit.* The adversary delights when our lives are complicated, complex, stressful, and confusing because when we feel this way, it is difficult, if not impossible, to feel the Spirit. It is Satan who would "keep us busily engaged in a multitude of trivial things in an effort to keep us distracted from the few vital things that make all the difference."[1]

I don't like the way I feel when I am filled with anxiety and stress. I recognize the "natural man" in me and know that I will feel this way until I can calm myself enough to be in tune with the Holy Ghost and able to listen to His promptings.

King Benjamin taught us that this is the way in which we will become saints—by putting off the natural man (see Mosiah 3:19), listening to the Holy Spirit, and accepting the Atonement of Jesus Christ.

I was sobered recently when I attended a study session on Carl Bloch's painting *Christ Healing the Sick at Bethesda*. I had never focused on this painting long enough to notice that only one person is looking at Christ—the infirm man, who has for years hoped that someone might lift him into the healing water. All the other people in the painting seem involved with each other or other things. They seem unaware that they are in the presence of Christ and that a great miracle is about to take place.

I began thinking of my own life. If I had been there, would I have been too busy with my own thoughts and activities that I would not have seen Christ? Do miracles pass us by or go unnoticed because we are too focused on our calendars instead of on our Christ? Sometimes the activities of our daily lives keep us so distracted from what really matters that our spiritual view is dulled as we focus on things that matter very little.

When I first began thinking about *simplification* more than two years ago, I thought primarily of finding ways to better organize my life. I read books about how to simplify—

to downsize, learn to say no, get along by doing with less. I thought about the direction we have received from Church leaders to simplify and reduce with respect to programs and activities and meetings. If such a process is good for the Church as an organization, might it not also be good for us as individual members. Our leaders have taught that this is so.[2]

Since those early beginnings to improve my life and make it increasingly more effective, I have come to believe that to simplify our lives goes beyond mere management of outside interferences, such as interrupting phone calls and hectic schedules; it is far more than organizing closets or cleaning out unwanted and unused things that clutter our homes. To simplify is about enhancing our ability to

> TO SIMPLIFY IS TO CARE FOR
>
> THE LIFE OF THE SOUL.

focus on things that *really* matter, to deliberately choose our priorities, and to refuse to let unimportant things take over the things of real importance.

For me, simplification has become much more about spiritual things than about temporal things. To simplify requires that we look at things in a different way, with a larger, even eternal, perspective. To simplify our lives is a spiritual quest; it is to "care . . . for the life of the soul" (D&C 101:37).

5

I have to admit that trying to simplify my own life is one of the greatest challenges I face. I am so easily distracted by a variety of things, many of which are good. But without real focus, I find that the spiritual nourishment of prayer, scripture study, temple worship, and taking time to ponder are easily crowded out by various things of much lesser value. On the other hand, when I put things of a spiritual nature first, other things in my life seem to go more smoothly and with minimal distractions.

My writing about simplification does *not* mean I've mastered the ability to simplify. I am convinced that learning to simplify is not a one-time activity; it is a lifetime endeavor.

Determining how to write a simple book about how to simplify life is not a simple thing! We are all so very different—by background, marital status, nationality, culture, opportunities for learning, income, size of families, friends, work, physical and emotional health, living conditions, and age. But I believe there are guiding principles that can be useful regardless of our circumstances.

To give guidance to my thoughts, I have used each letter of the word *simplify* to represent a principle that can help us begin to think about positive changes in our lives and then to make those changes.

s – stillness

i – integrity

m – mercy

p – prune

l – let go

i – impossible

f – fortify

y – you

May I also suggest a few guidelines as you begin this new adventure to care for the life of your soul and to simplify:

1. What appears simple is usually not easy.

2. There are many right ways to do things. In fact, there may be no right or wrong way to simplify your life. Yours is an individual quest.

3. Changing attitudes and ways of doing takes time. Do not create self-imposed deadlines.

4. It is impossible to add something to your life without taking something away. There are only twenty-four hours in a day, and most people in our society are already sleep deprived.

5. Introspection is critical to transformation.

6. Although many external conditions are beyond our control, we are always capable of making internal decisions.

7. Change is *always* possible. One of the most important things you can do is to ask our Heavenly Father, in prayer, what

you need to change and what steps you need to take to bring about this change.

8. This book is not for speed-reading. Choose a chapter, thought, or idea that has interest or meaning to you, think about it, and be sensitive to the promptings of the Holy Ghost. Too often we ignore thoughts and feelings that come to us when we read or hear an idea. Remember Christ's counsel: "Behold, I will tell you in your mind [thoughts] and in your heart [feelings], by the Holy Ghost. . . . this is the spirit of revelation" (D&C 8:2–3).

My prayer is that in the busyness of your life, you may find a thought or an idea from this book that will help you experience peace—the peace promised by the Prince of Peace, Him who stilled not only the waters but the hearts of the believers: "Peace I leave with you," He said, "my peace I give unto you: not as the world giveth, give I unto you. Let not your heart be troubled, neither let it be afraid" (John 14:27).

Be still, and know that
I am God.

—Psalm 46:10

two

One day on my way to the grocery store, I noticed a car in our ward meetinghouse parking lot. A woman was behind the wheel. Wondering if she might be having car problems, I drove up beside her car. The woman's head was down, and she looked as if she were crying. I debated whether or not to disturb her. I felt to knock gently on the car window, hoping not to startle her. She looked up and then rolled down her window. When I asked if there was anything I could do to help, she said, "Oh no. I just needed some peace and quiet."

I think she is not alone. There are times when each of us seeks for peace and quiet—for stillness.

Years ago I read Anne Morrow Lindbergh's book *Gift from the Sea*. In this short book, Lindbergh describes a brief vacation alone at a seashore, away from everyday distractions with time to reevaluate her life. She writes of the frustrations of her daily life—the things we all deal with, especially as women: maintaining and cleaning a home, planning meals, purchasing food, attending meetings, making telephone calls, carpooling, making and keeping doctor and dentist appointments, doing laundry, and on and on. "My mind reels with it," she writes. "What a circus act we women perform every day of our lives. It puts the trapeze artist to shame. This is not the life of simplicity but life of multiplicity that the wise men warn us of. It leads not to unification but to fragmentation. It does not bring grace; it destroys the soul."[1]

Anne Lindbergh wrote this book more than fifty years ago. What would she think of our lives today? They are not only noisier but much, much busier.

I remember envying Lindbergh as she enjoyed and learned from her brief, insightful vacation. What a luxury to be alone, to have time to think, to write, and to rest. I knew that would be impossible for me and for most of us. Then, while reading her book, I came across the phrase "islands in time."[2] I began thinking about creating an island *of* time, not somewhere on an exotic island but in my everyday life. Couldn't I carve out just a little time each day to experience time to be quiet, a time when I could just stop what I was doing and experience an island of time?

At the time I was a graduate student at Brigham Young University and also taught several classes. I watched students come running into class looking burdened with assignments and needing time to just catch their breath. One day I talked with them about this idea of creating an island of time. At the next class meeting, instead of beginning to teach immediately, I asked everyone to gather in a circle. We sat quietly for a moment, and then I shared a thought I had found that brought new insight and meaning to me. So many students commented on it that I decided to begin each class in this manner. Class members soon began to bring inspirational thoughts to share. Some thirty-five years later, I still on occasion meet former students. "Remember islands of time?" many have asked. "What wonderful times those were!"

Few, if any, of us have the time or means to escape to an island. But consider thinking of a time each day that you could call *your* island of time, a time when you could escape the busyness of daily responsibilities. The place matters little—it could even be in a car in a church parking lot. For others, it could be a quiet bench in a park, a library, a bedroom, or maybe even the bathroom. The place is not as important as the quiet you will find—quiet time to be still, to think, to breathe deeply, and to feel His peace.

We live in a world of sound—the ubiquitous ring of the cell phone, the television (which is often on even when no one is watching), radios, CDs, DVDs, stereo equipment, and home theaters. People are seen on streets and in offices "plugged in" to a CD player, MP3 device, or cell phone. Cars and homes can be equipped to provide surround sound. Making sound is *big* business!

> WHEN YOU ARE STILL, WONDERFUL THINGS WILL BEGIN TO HAPPEN IN YOUR LIFE. AS YOU CARE FOR THE LIFE OF YOUR SOUL, THINGS THAT SEEMED OVERWHELMING AND DIFFICULT WILL DIMINISH.

Some noise comes from just being in the world. Babies cry, children yell, dishwashers swish, glasses break, refrigerators hum, and people talk (often in loud voices). I think it of interest, and of no small import, that in a general conference as President Gordon B. Hinckley suggested that we all have room for improvement, he included, "We can lower our voices a few decibels."[3]

In today's world it is possible that we are *never* completely quiet—never in a place or state where we are able to block out all sound or noise. Likewise, we sometimes experience inner noise, thoughts that churn in our minds and which we seem unable to still.

As we think to simplify and make it a spiritual quest, we are reminded that the Lord commands us to be still and to listen. As Elijah learned, the Lord was to be heard not in the crashing of mountains, or wind, or earthquake but in a "still small voice" (1 Kings 19:12). The Nephites learned a similar truth. After the crucifixion of Christ and after tempests, earthquakes, fires, whirlwinds, physical upheavals, darkness, and finally silence, the people of Nephi heard a voice. "It was not a harsh voice, neither was it a loud voice; nevertheless, and notwithstanding it being a *small* voice it did pierce them that did hear to the center . . . and did cause their hearts to burn." Even then, it was not until "the third time they did understand the voice which they heard; and it said unto them: Behold my Beloved Son, in whom I am well pleased . . . hear ye him" (3 Nephi 11:3, 6–7; emphasis added).

The scriptures give us ample instruction about how the Spirit speaks to us, but to hear the still, small voice we must be still and listen. This was forcefully brought to my mind early one morning as I finished my prayers. I admit to being guilty of often jumping to my feet as I conclude a prayer with "amen." But on this particular morning I simply stayed on my knees and listened.

I had been praying, as I always did, for my father. He had suffered for many years from the effects of Parkinson's disease. As the disease progressed, he gradually lost his ability to speak, to eat, and to control bodily functions. In his prime, Dad had been a superintendent of schools, president of a variety of civic organizations, and a leader in the community and his church. To see him unable to do anything was almost more than I could bear. For years I included in every prayer I offered, "Please, don't let Dad suffer."

That morning when I stayed on my knees and listened, I gained an enormous insight—an eternal perspective. As if the Lord Himself stood beside me, words came clearly into my mind: "My Son suffered."

I recorded in my journal: "It almost took my breath away. I felt as if I had been 'taught from on high.' I began to pray that both Dad and I would be able to endure to the end." That experience led to a search of the scriptures. I wanted to know more about Christ's suffering and what is to be learned from suffering. I recorded each of the scripture references with a short note about what I had learned.

More than a year later, I felt impressed to share this

experience with Dad. Though he could not speak, I asked him, "Do you want me to read some of the scriptures I found?"

Sensing no objection, I began reading. At one point, I glanced up to look at Dad. Though he could not communicate verbally, there was an understanding and knowing look on his face.

"You know all of this, don't you?" I asked. "You 'get it.'"

Ever so slightly I thought I saw his head nod in recognition. I *knew* I saw his eyes smiling.

When I left that day, Dad did something he hadn't done for at least a year—he gave me our secret signal, squeezing my hand three times to indicate "I love you."

I could not have known as we parted that it would be the last time we would be together on this earth. Dad died only eight days later.

> WE ALL SEARCH FOR PEACE. IT IS ONE OF THE ULTIMATE QUESTS OF THE HUMAN SOUL.

Just as I needed personal revelation to understand my father's suffering, so we all need personal revelation for our own lives. President Boyd K. Packer told graduating students at Brigham Young University–Hawaii: "These are sobering times. . . . You won't survive spiritually, unless you know how to receive revelation." He, too, acknowledged that we live in a "noisy world" but added, "revelation comes in the quiet times. It will come when the Lord can speak to our feelings. . . . Go quietly," he counseled. "Go quietly into the world. Go quietly about your affairs, and learn that in the still, small hours of the morning the Lord will speak to you. He will never fail to answer your prayers."[4]

THESE ARE SOBERING TIMES.

. . . YOU WON'T SURVIVE

SPIRITUALLY, UNLESS

YOU KNOW HOW TO

RECEIVE REVELATION.

President Boyd K. Packer

Isn't it interesting that we always talk about "saying our prayers" and seldom, if ever, about "listening our prayers"? When we pray we communicate with our Heavenly Father. Often, we act as though prayer is a one-way communication. Praying to our Father should include listening. To *commune* is the root of *communicate* and *communion*. To commune with another means to *talk together* intimately; to be in close rapport.[5]

Prayer should not be a one-sided experience in which we do all the talking and then walk away. We need to learn to listen—to take note of thoughts and impressions that come into our minds and of the feelings we experience (see D&C

8:2). As we listen, He will speak to us, teach us, reassure us, and bless us.

These truths are taught in one of my favorite hymns, "Oh, May My Soul Commune with Thee":

Oh, may my soul commune with thee
And find thy holy peace;
From worldly care and pain of fear,
Please bring me sweet release.

Oh, bless me when I worship thee
To keep my heart in tune,
That I may hear thy still, small voice,
And, Lord, with thee commune.

Enfold me in thy quiet hour
And gently guide my mind
To seek thy will, to know thy ways,
And thy sweet Spirit find.

Lord, grant me thy abiding love
And make my turmoil cease.
Oh, may soul commune with thee
And find thy holy peace.[6]

I often find myself humming that hymn tune, and when I do, it is usually because I want my turmoil to be stilled so that I can find His holy peace. We all search for peace; it is one of the ultimate quests of the human soul. But it is so easy to let life "shallow us up," as if we had no control over ourselves, our response to situations, or the circumstances in which we find ourselves. We can always make choices. It was part of the reason the war in heaven was fought—so that we would have agency and be able "to act for [our]selves and not to be acted upon" (2 Nephi 2:26).

But we must act; we must choose what we will do. Virginia H. Pearce writes: "Taking time alone to think and pray is all too rare in a busy and fast-moving world. It just doesn't happen if it isn't consciously programmed into life." She tells of the time when their home was filled with children and there seemed to be no time to meditate. "But," she writes, "I found that on Mondays, if I were vigilant, I could find a way to have my own quiet time for reflection and renewal."[7]

Did you catch the phrase "consciously programmed"?

> TAKING TIME ALONE TO THINK AND PRAY IS ALL TOO RARE IN A BUSY AND FAST-MOVING WORLD. IT JUST DOESN'T HAPPEN IF IT ISN'T CONSCIOUSLY PROGRAMMED INTO LIFE.
>
> Virginia H. Pearce

We're not talking about *finding time* but rather about *making time,* making a choice to be still and listen. For most of us, this will require giving up something—perhaps a favorite TV program, "mindless" surfing of the Internet, or lengthy time chatting on the phone. We might also want to give thought to being more selective in what we read and learn to use the "delete" button on our computers more often.

One of the hardest things for me to do is to make myself pull away, to stop rushing around, frantically trying to accomplish the things that need doing. I find it so easy to get caught up in life, to do what others are doing, and to drift along, giving little thought to what I want or need to do to care for the life of *my* soul. Because I like to be in the action and not miss out on anything, it is difficult to pull away, out of the busyness and noise and confusion of everyday life. It is so easy to say to myself, "I just don't have time to be still and listen." I know I'm not the only one with that response. It is no wonder we need to consciously program time for "reflection and renewal."

Listen. Why is that so hard? *Be still.* At times this seems impossible, but I know from personal experience that being still is the only way I can still my mind and heart to feel the promptings of the Spirit. Often I will review in my mind these words:

I will not doubt, I will not fear;
God's love and strength are always near.
His promised gift helps me to find
An inner strength and peace of mind.
I give the Father willingly
My trust, my prayers, humility.
His Spirit guides; his love assures
That fear departs when faith endures.[8]

Following an especially hectic time, I recorded the following in my journal: "I wanted to just run away, but since that wasn't a possibility, I went into my office and locked the door. After humming the tune and thinking of the words to the hymn 'When Faith Endures,' I wonder why I am so slow to learn? When I finally got away by myself, I had the most overwhelming feeling of peace and a quiet confidence. I knew I was not alone. I was able to feel myself let go of anxiety and tension, to think clearly, to feel His Spirit, and gain insights that will help me complete the many assignments looming before me."

The idea of simplifying my life has been ever present in my mind since I returned from the New Zealand Wellington Mission several years ago. But before I could begin to write about it, I had to let the ideas season within me. I needed to talk with others about their experiences. And I needed to make sure I did not write about things that just sounded good; I needed to try things for myself, to live with them, to make sure that the principles I was writing about were sound and true.

From personal experience, I know it is possible to make time to be alone and to find a place where no one will interrupt you—even in your car, if need be. But it requires a conscious decision to do so. When you are still, wonderful things will begin to happen in your life. You will have an increased sense that as you care for the life of your soul, other things that seemed overwhelming and difficult will diminish.

GETTING STARTED

1. Consider where might be the best place for you to go to experience stillness.

2. When will be the best time? At first, you might only be able to find spare moments in a day or two a week. The important thing is to begin, even if it comes in snippets of time.

3. The amount of time is not important. It might be better to find a ten-minute block of time to be still than to decide being still is not possible because you don't have an extra hour in your schedule.

4. Don't go to your place of stillness, your own island of time, with any agenda except to be still, to do nothing, to sit quietly. Once you release your mind, the Lord can better guide your soul.

5. Take with you something to write on, for when you are still, God can speak to you.

6. To begin, read and think about one of the following quotations.

Scriptures and Thoughts to Ponder

President Gordon B. Hinckley: "We need to build ourselves spiritually. We live in a world of rush and go, of running here and there and in every direction. We are very busy people. We have so much to do. We need to get off by ourselves once in awhile and think of the spiritual things and build ourselves spiritually. If you have a study at home, lock yourselves in it. If you have a place in the basement where you can be by yourself, go there. Get by yourself and think of things of the Lord. . . . Just meditate and reflect . . . about yourself and your relationship to your Heavenly Father and your Redeemer. It will do something for you."[9]

Quiet times of revelation tune my heart to see
Tender mercies of the Lord are daily shown to me.
As I feel the love of God I seem to understand
I can be an instrument in Heav'nly Father's hands.
Quiet times of inspiration touch me and I feel
God's pure love is guiding me, His promises are real.
As I nurture those I love within my daily sphere
I feel strength beyond my own and know that God is
    near.
And when I feel His love, my heart has one desire;
To share the joy and warmth His perfect love inspires.
My hands reach out to all in purest charity
That other souls may feel His love through me.[10]

President James E. Faust: "We are bombarded on all sides by a vast number of messages we don't want or need. More information is generated in a single day than we can absorb in a lifetime. To fully enjoy life, all of us must find our own breathing space and peace of mind."[11]

President David O. McKay: "Meditation is the language of the soul. . . . Meditation is one of the most secret, most sacred doors through which we pass into the presence of the Lord. . . .

To have communication with God, through his Holy Spirit, is one of the noblest aspirations of life."[12]

When all around seems strange and wrong,
I seek to know what's right.
I pull away to be alone;
I seek to find the light.
The Spirit whispers; I feel at peace,
I know God cares and hears.
Eternal truth rings in my ears.
My soul no longer fears.

O Heav'nly Father, hear my prayer
And calm my troubled mind.
Help keep my thoughts in thee alone,
Eternal truths to find.
The Spirit whispers; I feel at peace.
I know God cares and hears.
Eternal truth rings in my ears.
My soul no longer fears.
. . . .
I feel at peace.

I feel at peace.

I feel at peace.[13]

"Let your hearts be comforted . . . for all flesh is in my hands; be still and know that I am God" (D&C 101:16).

"Stop, and stand still until I command thee, and I will provide means whereby thou mayest accomplish the thing which I have commanded thee" (D&C 5:34).

The New Testament contains numerous references to Christ's going up into a mountain, sometimes to pray, sometimes to simply be alone (see Matthew 5:1; 14:23; Mark 3:13; Luke 6:12; John 6:15). Mark 6:30–32 records that when the Apostles were with Jesus, they "told him all things, both what they had done, and what they had taught." After this reporting session, Christ said to them, "Come ye yourselves apart into a desert place, and rest a while: for there were many coming and going, and they had no leisure so much as to eat. And they departed into a desert place by ship privately."

*I, the Lord, love him because
of the integrity of his heart,
and because he loveth that
which is right before me.*

—Doctrine and Covenants 124:15

integrity

I love to look up words in Noah Webster's *American Dictionary of the English Language* published in 1828 because the
definitions given in that dictionary represent the meanings of
words as they were used in the days of the Prophet Joseph
Smith. This dictionary defines *integrity* as "wholeness; the
entire, unimpaired state of anything, particularly of the mind;
moral soundness, purity; honesty." Interestingly, the prime root
of the Hebrew word for *integrity*, as used in the Old Testament, means "complete" or "whole." This same root word is
used in the word Thummim (as in Urim and Thummim) and
means "complete truth or perfection."[1]

In *The Book of Virtues*, William Bennett discusses "Plato
on Justice," explaining that the ancient Greek word for *just*

can have a variety of meanings. Bennett suggests that Plato's *justice* is more like our understanding of *integrity*. He rephrases Plato's question, asking instead, "Why should I be a person of integrity?" and responds, "Because it is healthier. Integrity—having one's psychological parts *integrated,* 'having it all together' . . . is the sort of condition in which any really rational human being would choose to be . . . Acquiring integrity is getting one's person in shape."[2]

> ACQUIRING INTEGRITY
>
> IS GETTING ONE'S PERSON
>
> IN SHAPE.
>
> *William Bennett*

How is *integrity* related to *simplify*? Because we live in a time that often threatens the quality of being complete or whole—of having our inner selves in shape—the spiritual quest of living with integrity helps us care for the life of our souls.

We often hear such phrases as "I'm being pulled in too many directions" or "I feel fragmented." Sometimes we talk of "being stretched too thin" or "dealing with this issue just pulled me apart." When we feel we are being pushed or pulled in many directions, we do not experience wholeness. One of the ways we can simplify our lives is to live with integrity—to make our actions consistent with our beliefs.

The circles below represent beliefs and actions:

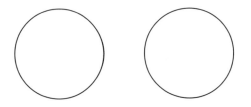

In this illustration beliefs and actions are far apart, not integrated. The farther away from each other our individual beliefs and actions are, the more "pulled apart" we feel. One of the tests of this life is to make our actions true to our beliefs—to become whole, at one with ourselves and God.

The illustration below represents integrity, a state in which beliefs and actions are integrated. This integration is integrity or wholeness.

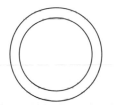

A number of years ago, the United States Department of Health and Human Services reported that "the U.S. has indeed become a nation of believers in the virtue of exercise. But," the study continued, "most citizens confine their practice to nothing more strenuous than pushing a shopping cart around a supermarket on Saturday morning or shoveling down a pint of ice cream while doing laps between the kitchen and the TV set."[3] In other words, most people (80 to 90 percent) recognized the importance of exercise, but their actions were not consistent with their beliefs. They were not living with integrity.

WHEN WE DEPART FROM WHO WE ARE AND FROM OUR KNOWLEDGE OF RIGHT AND WRONG, WE NOT ONLY COMPLICATE OUR LIVES BUT FEEL INCREASED STRESS AND OFTEN GUILT.

I believe that a principal cause of the disharmony and stress we so often experience is living our lives with duplicity—saying we believe one way but acting very differently. We cannot think one way and act another without experiencing disharmony and stress. It causes a conflicting battle within us. To act with integrity, we must make our actions consistent with our knowledge of right and wrong. If we are to care for the life of the soul, we must take care to live with integrity.

I remember teaching a class of Mia Maids a lesson about the temple. I was a fairly recent convert and had not yet been endowed, so I was especially nervous about giving this lesson. I went to the class fasting. I had pictures, quotations, and a special magnetic picture of the temple I'd made for each young woman. I concluded by bearing my testimony of the importance of temples, of the privilege of being able to go to the temple, and of my plans to be endowed in the temple a year from the day I was baptized. Feeling insecure about the topic, I left no time for questions, nor did I invite comments or leave time for discussion.

Although I had felt prepared to give the lesson, I was not prepared for what happened *after* the lesson. As soon as I sat down, one of the young women responded, "I don't believe anything you said!" I was so shocked I didn't know how to respond. I chose to act as if I hadn't heard her and called on someone for the closing prayer. By the time the prayer concluded and the young women were leaving, I recognized I hadn't handled this situation well at all. I nervously asked Andrea (not her real name) if she could stay for a minute.

"No," she responded in a disgusted way. "I have to get home—right now!"

After I went home, I thought about what I should do. Following prayer, I felt impressed to call Andrea and invite her to my home so we could talk about what she was feeling and why she had made the comment she did. To my surprise, she agreed to come! I became increasingly nervous as the time for her visit approached. With a prayer in my heart, I answered the doorbell. We chatted awkwardly until I finally asked, "Why did you say what you did in class today?"

In a sarcastic voice, Andrea responded, "If the temple is so wonderful and is everything you said it is, why do my parents never go? I know they were married in the temple. Once when I answered the phone, someone from the ward wanted to ask my dad to go to the temple for something special. When I told Dad what the call was about, he said, 'Tell them I'm not home.'"

I felt sick inside. Although I tried to reinforce all that I'd taught earlier in the day, it was one of those times when actions spoke louder than words. Andrea's parents could never have known how their lack of integrity would affect their daughter's feelings about the house of the Lord.

To live with integrity means we feel and live with wholeness. When we—whether consciously or unconsciously—depart from who we are and from our knowledge of right and wrong, we not only complicate our lives but feel increased stress and often guilt.

Have you ever been in a meeting when someone talked of the importance of daily scripture study? If this is something you believe in but are not doing, you begin to experience feelings of guilt or anxiety. You believe in studying the scriptures, you know you should be doing it, but your life has become so overscheduled that this important and sacred activity is too easily pushed to the side.

A simple exercise can help us check our personal integrity. Divide a piece of paper into halves. On one half of the paper write the word *actions*; on the other half, the word *beliefs*.

On the *action* side list the things you have done this past week (cooked meals, drove children to school, completed visiting teaching, visited a friend in the hospital, cleaned the pantry, and so on).

On the *beliefs* side of the paper, list the things you believe in, the things you value and desire to do in your life.

How do these two lists compare? Do your actions match your beliefs?

If they do, you probably already have the confidence that a life of integrity brings—you feel whole, complete, and at peace.

If there is a discrepancy between your actions and beliefs, you might feel disquieted, agitated, or depressed. Here, then, is your opportunity to make some changes, to look at ways in which you can make time to care for your soul.

It is challenging for me to say no to things, especially when I'm asked to give a talk or teach a class—both of which I enjoy doing. I'm learning how many of those things I'm able to do while maintaining my physical and emotional health and attending to other responsibilities (beliefs), but often I let my ego dictate my actions. Such dilemmas are hard for me, but when my actions are consistent with my beliefs, I am happier, healthier, and much more at peace. I know that when we live with integrity, we will experience peace. That in itself will reassure us that we are living our beliefs.

What powerful examples we have in the scriptures of people acting with integrity! Only a few days after fourteen-year-old Joseph Smith saw the Father and the Son, he shared his experience with some ministers. They told him his vision was "of the devil, that there were no such things as visions or revelations in these days." He wrote of experiencing great prejudice, bitter persecution, and backbiting. He compared himself to Paul, who stood before King Agrippa, in telling his account of seeing a light and hearing a voice, "but still there were but few who believed him; some said he was dishonest, others said he was mad." And yet, Joseph wrote, "[Paul] had seen a vision, he knew he had, and all the persecution under heaven could not make it otherwise" (Joseph Smith–History 1:21, 24).

Likewise, Joseph Smith wrote of his experience: "Why persecute me for telling the truth? I have actually seen a vision; and who am I that I can withstand God, or why does the world think to make me deny what I have actually seen? For I had seen a vision; I knew it, and I knew that God knew it, and I could not deny it" (Joseph Smith–History 1:25). The footnote by the word "deny" in this verse refers us to the following words in the Topical Guide: *courage, honesty,* and *integrity.* Without question, fourteen-year-old Joseph Smith acted with integrity.

The prophet Abinadi prophesied before King Noah and his wicked priests about the coming of Christ. His words engendered such anger among them that after consulting with his priests for three days, Noah told Abinadi, "We have found an accusation against thee, and thou art worthy of death." But the king gave Abinadi a way out: he could preserve his life if he would recall all the words he had spoken against King Noah and his people. With courage and integrity, Abinadi said, "I will not recall the words which I have spoken . . . for they are true. . . . I will suffer even until death, and I will not recall my words." When he continued to testify against King Noah, the king became fearful and was about to release him, "but the priests lifted up their voices against [Abinadi]", and

THE SPIRITUAL QUEST TO LIVE WITH INTEGRITY HELPS US CARE FOR THE LIFE OF OUR SOULS.

the king delivered him to be slain. Immediately, Abinadi was bound, scourged, and suffered death by fire. The scriptures record that he was put to death by fire "because he *would not* deny the commandments of God" (Mosiah 17:7, 9–10, 12, 20; emphasis added).

I have heard people say that they believe some things so strongly they would be willing to die for these beliefs. Although few, if any, of us will be required to die for what we believe, *living* what we believe brings wholeness of body, mind, and spirit. In that wholeness we find peace.

The lack of integrity in daily living is sometimes painfully obvious. "Everybody's doing it" is a favorite line of some whining children. Cheating is becoming increasingly "acceptable." In 2005, Don McCabe of The Center for Academic Integrity released a report of a multiyear survey of almost fifty thousand undergraduate students across more than sixty campuses. He found the following:

"On most campuses, 70% of students admit to some cheating. Close to one-quarter of the participating students admitted to serious test cheating in the past year and half admitted to one or more instances of serious cheating on written assignments. . . . Studies of 18,000 students at 61 schools, conducted in the last four years, suggest cheating is also a significant problem in high school—over 70% of respondents at public and parochial schools admitted to one or more instances of serious test cheating and over 60% admitted to some form of plagiarism. . . . About half of all students admitted they had engaged in some level of plagiarism using the Internet."[4]

These statistics are lamentable. They echo the dishonesty that has seemed rampant in some businesses where trusting employees and stockholders are fed lies and false information, all to the greed and dishonor of another. Integrity is as vital an economic principle as it is a character trait.

But integrity can often slip in more subtle ways. There are times we may tell ourselves, "It's only a little thing. Who will know?" We may give in to a friend's request to copy a computer program that has been licensed only for our own use. We may violate copyright laws by copying music or movies, justifying to ourselves that it really doesn't matter, and anyway, who will ever know? A practice that is becoming increasingly popular among college students is submitting term papers obtained largely from Internet "term-paper mills." We need to check ourselves by making sure we give appropriate credit for an idea, a phrase, or a quotation we use in lessons or talks or writings.

It is a serious matter when our lives (actions) are out of harmony with the gospel principles (beliefs) we profess. The consequences of our behavior, while perhaps not known by anyone else, should be of grave concern to us. President Gordon B. Hinckley has challenged us to "rise above the evils of the world," while reminding us that "it is a challenge to work in the world and live above its filth." He says, "Be strong. . . . let our personal *integrity,* our sense of right and wrong, and simple honesty govern our actions."[5]

A friend of President James E. Faust related an "experience her husband had while attending medical school. 'Getting into medical school is pretty competitive, and the desire to do well and be successful puts a great deal of pressure on the new incoming freshmen. My husband had worked hard on his studies and went to attend his first examination. The honor system was expected behavior at the medical school. The professor passed out the examination and left the room. Within a short time, students started to pull little cheat papers out from under their papers or from their pockets. My husband recalled his heart beginning to pound as he realized it is pretty hard to compete against cheaters. About that time a tall, lanky student stood up in the back of the room and stated: "I left my hometown and put my wife and three little babies in an upstairs apartment and worked very hard to get into medical school. And I'll turn in the first one of you who cheats, and *you better believe it!*" They believed it. There were many sheepish expressions, and those cheat papers started to disappear as fast as they had appeared. He set a standard for the class which eventually graduated the largest group in the school's history.'

"The young, lanky medical student who challenged the cheaters was J Ballard Washburn, who became a respected physician and in later years received special recognition from the Utah Medical Association for his outstanding service as a medical doctor. He also served as a General Authority and . . . president of the Las Vegas Nevada Temple."⁶

In 1856, President Heber C. Kimball told the people: "The time is coming when we will be mixed up in these now peaceful valleys to that extent that it will be difficult to tell the face of a Saint from the face of an enemy to the people of God. Then . . . look out for the great sieve, for there will be a great sifting time, and many will fall; for I say unto you there is a *test*, a TEST, a TEST coming, and who will be able to stand?"⁷

Referencing this quotation, President Gordon B. Hinckley wrote: "I do not know the precise nature of that test. But I am inclined to think the time is here and that the test lies in our capacity *to live the gospel* rather than adopt the ways of the world.

"I do not advocate a retreat from society. On the contrary, we have a responsibility and a challenge to take our places in the world. . . . But this does not require a surrender of standards.

"We can maintain the *integrity* of our families if we will follow the counsel of our leaders. As we do so, those about us will observe with respect and be led to inquire how it is done. . . .

". . . Beginning with you and me, there can be an entire people who by the virtue of our lives in our homes, in our vocations, even in our amusements, can become as a city upon a hill to which men may look and learn, and an ensign to the nations from which the people of the earth may gather strength."[8]

Hyrum Smith was acknowledged, blessed, and loved by the Lord because of the "integrity of his heart" (D&C 124:15). In our society, we hear increasing reports of fraud, false advertising, white collar crime, cheating, disregard for copyright laws, and other forms of dishonesty. As we commit to making our actions consistent with our beliefs, we will not only enjoy the fruits of an honest life but will take a step closer to caring for the life of our souls and simplifying our lives.

GETTING STARTED

1. Try listing your actions of the past week and comparing them with what you truly believe. Determine if you need to make changes. If you do, consider just one thing you might alter that would bring your actions closer to your beliefs.

2. I've mentioned a few forms of cheating that are often seen as acceptable. There are many, many more. Such simple things as taking pens or other office supplies from your work place for use at home cheats your employer. Using the church or office copy machine to make personal copies is stealing. Making personal phone calls on company time robs others of your service and robs you of your integrity. Being dishonest about expenditures on your income tax is lying. As you ponder the concept of integrity, search your heart for areas of behavior you want to change.

3. Resolve to do what the Savior would do in connection with everything you read, watch, and listen to. Read Moroni 10:32 and think about what it means to "deny yourselves of all ungodliness." For two weeks eliminate actions that could be offensive to the Spirit of God. This may mean eliminating certain movies, music, television programs, videos, literature, conversations, and actions. Make it a habit to do what the Savior would want you to do.

4. When you arrive late at home or for a meeting, do you sometimes make excuses or exaggerate the truth to justify your lateness? Be mindful of such behavior and commit to act with increased integrity the next time.

Scriptures and Thoughts to Ponder

Karl G. Maeser: "I have been asked what I mean by word of honor. I will tell you. Place me behind prison walls—walls of stone ever so high, ever so thick, reaching ever so far into the ground—there is a possibility that in some way or another I may be able to escape; but stand me on the floor and draw a chalk line around me and have me give my word of honor never to cross it. Can I get out of the circle? No, never! I'd die first!"[9]

The year before his tragic death in 1865, Abraham Lincoln stated to a committee: "I desire so to conduct the affairs of this administration that if at the end, when I come to lay down the reins of power, I have lost every friend on earth, I shall at least have one friend left, and that friend shall be down inside of me."[10]

President Spencer W. Kimball: "Integrity may be defined as a state or quality of being complete, undivided or unbroken, wholeness and unimpaired, purity and moral soundness; it is unadulterated genuineness and deep sincerity. . . .

"Self-justification is the enemy to repentance. God's

spirit continues with the honest in heart to strengthen, to help, and to save, but invariably the Spirit of God ceases to strive with the man who 'excuses' himself in his wrong doing.

"Practically all dishonesty owes its continued existence and growth to this inward distortion we call 'self-justification.' It is the first, the worst, and the most insidious and damaging form of cheating—cheating our-selves."[11]

SELF-JUSTIFICATION . . .

IS THE FIRST, THE WORST,

AND THE MOST INSIDIOUS

AND DAMAGING FORM

OF CHEATING—

CHEATING OURSELVES.

President Spencer W. Kimball

President Gordon B. Hinckley: "It is not easy to be honest when all about you there are those who are inter-ested only in making 'a fast buck.' It is not always easy to be temperate when all about you there are those who scoff at sobriety. It is not easy to be industrious when all about you there are those who do not believe in the value of work. It is not easy to be a man of integrity when all about you there are those who will forsake principle for expediency.

". . . A man has to live with his principles. A man has to live with his convictions. A man has to live with his testimony.

Unless he does so, he is miserable—dreadfully miserable. And while there may be thorns, while there may be disappointment, while there may be trouble and travail, heartache and heartbreak, and desperate loneliness, there will be peace and comfort and strength."[12]

Jeb McGruder: "Somewhere between my ambition and my ideals, I lost my ethical compass."[13]

Read in the following passages of scripture about individuals who showed integrity: Genesis 39; Daniel 3:8–25; 6:1–23; Doctrine and Covenants 124:15, 20.

William Shakespeare: "If I lose mine honour, I lose myself."[14]

Blessed are the merciful:
for they shall obtain mercy.

—Matthew 5:7

mercy

four

Probably no other book on the subject of simplifying includes a chapter on mercy. So why is there one in this book? Because, as we examine ways we might enhance our ability to simplify our lives, we are looking to reduce and eventually to eliminate things that distract us from the things of eternal consequence. We desire to increase our ability to focus on things that really matter, to deliberately choose our priorities, and to refuse to let unimportant things take over things of real importance. Simplifying is not just dealing with things of a temporal nature. To truly simplify is a spiritual quest. We are about much more than managing stressful schedules or cleaning out cluttered closets. We are learning to care for the life of our souls.

Too many among us hold grudges and ill feelings toward others for the way they treated us or for something they said about which we chose to take offense. At times we hear comments like "Well, I'm never going to forgive her for what she did to me!"

"Such an attitude," President Thomas S. Monson has taught, "is destructive to an individual's well-being. It can canker the soul and ruin one's life." Concerning people who can forgive others but not themselves, President Monson added, "Such a situation is even more destructive."[1]

As we strive to simplify our lives and care for the life of our souls, we cannot allow such destructive forces to pull us down or keep us churned up or distracted. Such attitudes generate negativity, drain us of energy, and exhaust us emotionally.

My first experience with mercy, though I would not even have known the word, was when I was about six years old. I loved playing with marbles. I delighted in collecting and trading these beautifully colored and varied glass balls of different sizes. On this particular day, Dad had just come home from work. He sat down to read the evening paper, but I wanted him to play marbles with me. I can't remember exactly how my begging went, but when I got little response, I began lightly tossing the marbles, one at a time, against the outstretched newspaper he was holding in front of his face. I was totally ignored, which only added to my impatience and determination to get Dad's attention.

I began throwing the marbles harder and higher. All of a sudden I heard a terrible noise. Dad didn't have to put the newspaper down for me to know what had happened. I had thrown a marble hard enough and high enough to hit Dad's glasses. As he lowered the paper, I saw that one lens was shattered.

Dad didn't say anything. He just looked at me and then got up and left the room. Why didn't he spank me or lecture me? Why didn't he say something? I knew we weren't rich; how would he pay for new glasses? How would I pay for them? How would he see to do his work? I was in agony. I went to my room and stayed there until Mother called me for supper. I wasn't hungry, but I was given no choice about sitting at the table.

After we said grace, there was silence. Finally Dad spoke. "Tell Mother about the marble game you played today." I thought I would die as I sobbed my way through the stupid thing I had done. Finally, Dad told me to come and sit on his lap. I cried and cried as I tried to tell him how sorry I was for what I had done. He put his arms around me and quietly asked, "What did you learn from what happened?"

I don't remember my answer, but I do remember Dad's

response: "Now, you learned a good lesson today. You don't throw marbles in people's faces. I forgive you. I'll wear my old glasses for now. Let's forget about what happened and eat our supper. After a while, we'll go down to the Dairy Queen for some soft-serve ice cream."

Of course, I didn't know anything about mercy and justice at that young age. But I surely did feel Dad's forgiveness and his love for me. It is an incident I have never forgotten. My dad was a kind and generous man. That day I learned he was also merciful.

When I think of mercy, I recall the first time I learned an interesting pattern about the word *mercy* in the Book of Mormon. It is used in the very first book (1 Nephi 1), the last book (Moroni 10), and in approximately the middle of the Book of Mormon (Alma 33).

Nephi explains the purpose of the Book of Mormon: "Behold, I, Nephi, will show unto you that the tender mercies of the Lord are over all those whom he hath chosen, because of their faith, to make them mighty even unto the power of deliverance" (1 Nephi 1:20).

In the last book Moroni writes, "Behold, I would exhort you that when ye shall read these things, if it be wisdom in God that ye should read them, that ye would remember how merciful the Lord hath been unto the children of men, from the creation of Adam even down until the time that ye shall receive these things, and ponder it in your hearts" (Moroni 10:3). "Ponder *it* in your hearts." What are we to ponder? "How merciful the Lord hath been unto the children of men," including each of us.

In the middle of the Book of Mormon, Alma bears testimony of the merciful nature of God's Son and quotes the words of the prophet Zenock, who speaks of mercy in a very different way. Zenock said, "Thou art angry, O Lord, with this people, because they will not understand thy mercies which thou hast bestowed upon them because of thy Son" (Alma 33:16). Of all the reasons why the Lord might be angry with us, have you ever considered that it would be because we have not understood the mercies that are available to us through the Atonement of Jesus Christ? When I read this scripture, I am sobered and feel to give thanks to Heavenly Father for the great gift of His Son, Jesus Christ.

> HOW CAN WE EXPECT
>
> [MERCY] UNLESS WE HAVE
>
> BEEN MERCIFUL OURSELVES?
>
> *President Gordon B. Hinckley*

President Gordon B. Hinckley has talked about mercy as a godlike quality. "It is part of the endowment each of us receives as a son or daughter of God and partaker of a divine birthright. I plead for an effort among all of us to give greater expression and wider latitude to this instinct which lies within us. I am convinced that there comes a time, possibly many times, within our lives when we might cry out for mercy on the part of others. *How can we expect [mercy] unless we have been merciful ourselves?*[2] That is a sobering question.

Do you remember Christ's parable of the beggar Lazarus and the rich man?

> There was a certain rich man, which was clothed in purple and fine linen, and fared sumptuously every day:
>
> And there was a certain beggar named Lazarus, which was laid at his gate, full of sores,
>
> And desiring to be fed with the crumbs which fell from the rich man's table. . . .
>
> And it came to pass, that the beggar died, and was carried by the angels into Abraham's bosom: the rich man also died, and was buried;
>
> And in hell he lift up his eyes, being in torments, and seeth Abraham afar off, and Lazarus in his bosom.
>
> And he cried and said, Father Abraham, have

mercy on me, and send Lazarus, that he may dip the tip of his finger in water, and cool my tongue; for I am tormented in this flame.

But Abraham said, Son, remember that thou in thy lifetime receivedst thy good things, and likewise Lazarus evil things: but now he is comforted, and thou art tormented.

And beside all this, between us and you there is a great gulf fixed: so that they which would pass from hence to you cannot; neither can they pass to us, that would come from thence. (Luke 16:19–26)

We need not suffer as did the rich man, for the promise given by Christ is sure: *if we are merciful, we shall obtain mercy* (see Matthew 5:7). But it is so easy to become part of the world in which we live, a world filled with meanness, criticism, hostility, harshness, argumentation, faultfinding, anger, litigation, civil strife, and conflict. Many live with the attitude of an eye for an eye and a tooth for a tooth. Television programs show family arguments and fights. The media often mercilessly attacks politicians and church or civil leaders. Many feel they have been cheated or betrayed. If we harbor such feelings, we allow great damage to be done to our souls and we experience constant emotional turmoil.

My favorite 1828 dictionary defines *mercy* in a beautiful way: "That benevolence, mildness or tenderness of heart which disposes a person to overlook injuries, or to treat an offender better than he deserves; the disposition that tempers justice, induces an injured person to forgive trespasses and injuries, and to forbear punishment, or inflict less than law or justice will warrant. In this sense, there is perhaps no word in our language precisely synonymous with mercy."[3]

Think what could happen in our homes and neighborhoods if we determined to respond to others with mercy, to give others the benefit of the doubt, to resolve not to take offense when it is directed at us. When we hold grudges or ill-feelings toward another, harbor jealousies and anger, respond in critical or attacking ways, or simply withhold mercy toward others, we become burdened and emotionally drained. Imagine what our homes, places of business, grocery stores, schools, freeways, and even our chapels would be like if everyone practiced mercy toward others.

President Hinckley has said: "Mercy is the very essence of the gospel of Jesus Christ. The degree to which each of us is able to extend it becomes an expression of the reality of our discipleship under Him who is our Lord and Master."[4]

But often we want justice. Justice cries out, "It isn't fair." "Too bad for you—you're only getting what you deserve." "You expect me to work with her? Not after the way she's treated me!"

Elder Dallin H. Oaks told of an event that occurred in a firm where he once practiced law. A politician had been indicted for stuffing ballot boxes and asked a partner in the firm "to represent him in his criminal trial.

"'What can you do for me?' he asked. [The] partner replied that if this client retained our firm to conduct his defense, we would investigate the facts, research the law, and present the defense at the trial. 'In this way,' the lawyer concluded, 'we will get you a fair trial.'

"The politician promptly stood up, put on his hat, and stalked out of the office. Pursuing him down the hall, the lawyer asked what he had said to offend him. 'Nothing,' the politician replied. 'Then why are you leaving?' the lawyer asked. 'The odds aren't good enough,' the politician answered.

"That man would not retain our firm to represent him in court because we would only promise him a fair trial, and he knew he needed more than that. He knew he was guilty, and he could only be saved from prison by something more favorable to him than justice."[5]

In a way, aren't we all like this man, who has done something wrong, in wanting something more favorable to us than justice? Don't all of us want mercy? One of the crowning doctrines of the gospel is that because of the Atonement of the Son of God, we can, through faith in Jesus Christ and repentance, receive mercy. We will receive more than we deserve.

Elder Oaks explains: "The Atonement is the means by which justice is served and mercy is extended. In combination, justice and mercy and the Atonement constitute the glorious eternal wholeness of the justice and mercy of God."[6]

So how is mercy related to simplifying our lives and caring for our souls? First, we can make the world a better place by extending mercy to others. We can unburden ourselves of negative feelings that drain us emotionally, feelings of anger, resentment, criticism, and hostility. Second, we can seek forgiveness so we will not be weighed down by sin, so we will not destroy our inner peace, our souls.

A very dear friend has given me permission to share her story of seeking forgiveness, experiencing mercy, and being freed from sin. Her story began when she nervously called her bishop for an appointment to talk with him as soon as possible. He sensed her anxiety and agreed to meet her in his church office in fifteen minutes. Through tears and with great emotion, she confessed a sin with which she had been plagued for many years. She held her temple recommend in her shaking hand. When she finished pouring out her heart, she held up her recommend, saying, "I'm not worthy to have this."

For the first time, the bishop spoke. "You keep it," he said. "You will be much harder on yourself than I would be. Refrain from taking the sacrament for two weeks, and don't use your temple recommend for two weeks." Then he added, "Isn't it true, 'the natural man is an enemy to God,' but what a great blessing that through the Atonement of Christ we can become Saints?"

Tears flowed freely, down both my friend's face and the face of her bishop. Mercy had been extended; mercy was felt.

Periodically during the next two weeks, the bishop called to inquire how she was doing. On the evening before she would be able to once again use her temple recommend, she received an unexpected call from her bishop. "I've been thinking," he said, "how would you feel if I went to the temple with you? We could do baptisms. With you as proxy, I would be privileged to perform the ordinance."

They met the next morning in the baptistery of the temple to perform this saving ordinance of being washed clean from sin and past misdeeds. After the first proxy baptism was performed, tears mingling with water, my friend said quietly, "I am clean. I am clean." Quietly, the merciful bishop responded, "Yes, you are clean indeed."[7]

Without disclosing the transgression, my friend spoke to me of the great burden she had felt for many, many years.

She admitted to being embarrassed to discuss her problem with anyone, but finally she felt she could carry the burden no longer. "Relief, relief," she kept repeating, "I feel such relief. Why didn't I take care of this before?"

I thought how much lighter she must feel—a true indication of simplifying her life. But even more importantly, she had attended to and taken care of her soul.

Unrepented sin has a way of constantly nagging at us, even when we try to put the sin out of our minds. Sin holds us back, makes us think we aren't good enough, and tells us that God couldn't possibly love us because of what we've done. Nothing could be further from the truth!

All of us make mistakes, even tragic mistakes. In response to the frequently asked question, "Can I *ever* be forgiven?" President Boyd K. Packer said, "The answer is *yes!* The gospel teaches us that relief from torment and guilt can be earned through repentance. Save for those few who defect to perdition after having known a fulness, there is no habit, no addiction, no rebellion, no transgression, no offense exempted from the promise of complete forgiveness."[8]

Likewise, the Prophet Joseph Smith said, "There is never a time when the spirit is too old to approach God. All are within the reach of *pardoning mercy*."[9]

Too often we live with unrepented sin; our hearts are

heavy, our minds occupied with thoughts of past transgression. We carry burdens that weigh down our lives and make our lives more complex. There is such an easy answer to dealing with sin while at the same time simplifying our lives and caring for the life of our souls. The answer is Repentance. This is one of the most beautiful doctrines of the gospel. The Bible Dictionary teaches that repentance means "a turning of the heart and will to God."[10] In other words, we *want* to do what is right, to straighten out our lives with God, and to feel His peace.

I often share a personal experience that illustrates the concept of repentance—of turning and going in the right direction. Because I am terrible with directions, I had asked the Young Women president in whose stake I was speaking if she could send me a detailed map. Detailed it was! She not only drew a map but also wrote detailed directions, including things like "when you cross the railroad track

> SAVE FOR THOSE FEW WHO DEFECT TO PERDITION AFTER HAVING KNOWN A FULNESS, THERE IS NO HABIT, NO ADDICTION, NO REBELLION, NO TRANSGRESSION, NO OFFENSE EXEMPTED FROM THE PROMISE OF COMPLETE FORGIVENESS.
>
> *President Boyd K. Packer*

there will be an Albertson's grocery on the right side of the road. Two blocks later, there will be a Sinclair station on the left side of the road."

How could I go wrong? As I neared my destination, I took a last look at the map: there were two major turns, and I wanted to make sure I didn't miss them, especially as dusk was approaching. All of a sudden I had a funny feeling. I sensed I was driving in the wrong direction. I did what you would have done—stopped, turned on the overhead light, and looked at the map. Sure enough, I had missed a turn. I immediately turned around and quickly got back on the right road, arriving in ample time for the speaking engagement.

> THERE IS NEVER A TIME
> WHEN THE SPIRIT IS TOO OLD
> TO APPROACH GOD. ALL ARE
> WITHIN THE REACH OF
> PARDONING MERCY.
>
> *Joseph Smith*

I believe repentance is like that. Scriptures and living prophets provide the road map. When we read or receive counsel, if we recognize we are headed down the wrong road, we need to repent—we need to stop the behavior, turn around, and head in the right direction.

Fortunately, when I made the U-turn, I didn't go into the

ditch. If I had, I certainly wouldn't have just stayed there feeling sorry for myself. I would have walked to the nearest farmhouse for help, or if this had happened more recently, made a call on my cell phone. Help is always available. In the case of some sins, we need the bishop's help to "pull us out of the ditch." If you are in a ditch, go for help! If you are able to make a U-turn on your own, go to the Lord, acknowledge your wrongdoing, seek His forgiveness, and commit to staying on the right road.

Recently, as I read a talk given by Kim B. Clark, president of Brigham Young University–Idaho, I sensed a need to raise my level of personal righteousness. I began, almost subconsciously, to identify things I needed to do better, things I needed to stop doing. I knew I needed to make a U-turn in some areas of my life to turn back to God. That night my prayer was a prayer of repentance as I asked for forgiveness, help to make a turn toward God, and with His help, to become more righteous.[11]

So clearly and so simply the Lord invites, "Will ye not now return unto me, and repent of your sins . . . that I may heal you? . . . Behold, mine arm of mercy is extended towards you, and whosoever will come, him will I receive; and blessed are those who come unto me" (3 Nephi 9:13–14).

Jesus Christ Himself invites us, "*Let not your heart be*

troubled, neither let it be afraid" (John 14:27; emphasis added). Of that scripture, Elder Jeffrey R. Holland says: "That may be one of the Savior's commandments that is, even in the hearts of otherwise faithful Latter-day Saints, almost universally disobeyed; and yet I wonder whether our resistance to this invitation could be any more grievous to the Lord's merciful heart. . . . I am convinced that none of us can appreciate how deeply it wounds the loving heart of the Savior of the world when he finds that his people do not feel confident in his care or secure in his hands or trust in his commandments."[12]

The Savior taught, "Be ye therefore merciful, as your Father also is merciful" (Luke 6:36). Extending such mercy not only will bring peace to our lives and our souls but has the possibility of touching the hearts of others, giving them peace, and making the world a better place. Just as Dad held me on his lap and forgave me for what I had done, the Savior promises to forgive us. He is merciful in forgiving our sins as we forgive others and come unto Him seeking forgiveness and desiring to do better.

GETTING STARTED

1. Identify a time when you have been critical, judgmental, or harsh. If the same situation arose again, how would you handle it in a more merciful way?

2. How can you teach about mercy in your home?

3. Repent of trespasses or sins that are burdening you. If necessary, visit with your bishop.

4. Memorize several scriptures or other quotations about mercy.

Scriptures and Thoughts to Ponder

"For I will be merciful to their unrighteousness, and their sins and their iniquities will I remember no more" (Hebrews 8:12).

William Shakespeare:

> The quality of mercy is not strain'd,
> It droppeth as the gentle rain from heaven
> Upon the place beneath: it is twice blest;
> It blesseth him that gives, and him that takes. . . .
> It is an attribute to God himself.[13]

President Gordon B. Hinckley: "Let us be more merciful. . . . Let us be more compassionate, gentler, filled with forbearance and patience and a greater measure of respect one for another. In so doing, our very example will cause others to be more merciful, and we shall have greater claim upon the mercy of God who in His love will be generous toward us."[14]

President Boyd K. Packer: "So many live with accusing guilt when relief is ever at hand. So many are like the immigrant woman who skimped and saved and deprived herself until, by selling all of her possessions, she bought a steerage-class ticket to America.

"She rationed out the meager provisions she was able to bring with her. Even so, they were gone early in the voyage. When others went for their meals, she stayed below deck—determined to suffer through it. Finally, on the last day, she must, she thought, afford one meal to give her strength for the journey yet ahead. When she asked what the meal would cost, she was told that all of the meals had been included in the price of her ticket."[15]

Cast thy burden upon the Lord,
And he shall sustain thee.

He never will suffer the righteous to fall.
He is at thy right hand.
Thy mercy, Lord, is great
And far above the heav'ns.
Let none be made ashamed
That wait upon thee.[16]

"I know that thou are redeemed, because of the righteousness of thy Redeemer; for thou hast beheld that in the fulness of time he cometh to bring salvation unto men" (2 Nephi 2:3).

Elder Marion D. Hanks: "[The Lord] waits to be gracious! He loves to be merciful! The prophets call him 'the Father of mercies.' (2 Cor. 1:3.) They speak of his 'abundant mercy' (1 Pet. 1:3). . . . They declare his 'wisdom . . . mercy, and grace.' (2 Ne. 9:8.) And crowning all of this is the testimony that our Father 'delighteth in mercy.' (Micah 7:18.)"[17]

Lay aside the things of this world, and seek for the things of a better.

—Doctrine and Covenants 25:10

prune

five

Shortly after joining the Church, I heard the story of the currant bush as told by Hugh B. Brown, who served for many years as a member of the First Presidency and as a member of the Quorum of the Twelve Apostles. He used this personal experience to teach that God is the gardener and He knows what is best for us.

Elder Brown told of purchasing a rundown farm. One day he noticed a currant bush that had grown more than six feet high. The bush had no blossoms and currants. Having been raised on a fruit farm, he recognized the problem, got his pruning shears, and went to work. He clipped it back until there was nothing left but stumps.

"It was just coming daylight, and I thought I saw on top

of each of these little stumps what appeared to be a tear, and I thought the currant bush was crying. . . . And I looked at it and smiled and said, 'What are you crying about?' You know, I thought I heard that currant bush say this:

"'I was making such wonderful growth. I was almost as big as the shade tree and the fruit tree that are inside the fence, and now you have cut me down. Every plant in the garden will look down on me because I didn't make what I should have made. How could you do this to me? I thought you were the gardener here.'

" . . . I said, 'Look, little currant bush, I am the gardener here, and I know what I want you to be. I didn't intend you to be a fruit tree or a shade tree. I want you to be a currant bush, and someday, little currant bush, when you are laden with fruit, you are going to say, "Thank you, Mr. Gardener, for loving me enough to cut me down. Thank you, Mr. Gardener."'"

Elder Brown went on to tell of an event in his life many years later when he felt like the currant bush. He was in England in the Canadian Army. After working very hard, he learned he had not received an expected promotion. He related: "I was so bitter that I threw my hat on the cot. I clenched my fists, and I shook them at heaven. I said, 'How could you do this to me, God? I have done everything I could do to measure up. There is nothing that I could have done—that I should have done—that I haven't done. How could you do this to me?' I was as bitter as gall.

"And then I heard a voice, and I recognized the tone of this voice. It was my own voice, and the voice said, 'I am the gardener here. I know what I want you to do.'"

Immediately humbled, Elder Brown said, he knelt by his cot to ask forgiveness for his bitterness and ungratefulness. While still on his knees, he heard a group of Mormon army men singing:

> *But if, by a still, small voice he calls*
> *To paths that I do not know,*
> *I'll answer, dear Lord, with my hand in thine:*
> *I'll go where you want me to go.*
> (Hymns, *no. 270*)

Elder Brown said he arose from his knees a humble man. Then, in conclusion, he observed: "Many of you are going to have very difficult experiences: disappointment, heartbreak, bereavement, defeat. You are going to be tested and tried. I just want you to know that if you don't get what you think you ought to get, remember, God is the gardener here. He knows what He wants you to be. Submit yourselves to His will. Be worthy of His blessings, and you will get His blessings."[1]

For some reason, when I first heard this story, it seemed harsh and cruel to me. In hindsight, I wonder if I responded in this way because I had such limited knowledge of the gospel and no experience at all with pruning bushes or trees. Since first hearing the story more than thirty-five years ago, I've had many opportunities to prune bushes and trees. More important, I have repeatedly recognized the hand of the gentle Master Gardener carefully shaping me as I have sometimes felt the sharpness of the pruning shears.

I believe pruning has many applications as we think about simplifying our lives and caring for the life of our souls. It seems that way especially when I review some of the synonyms of the word *prune*: cut back, eliminate, exclude, pare down, reduce, shape.[2]

By no stretch of the imagination am I an expert gardener, but I have learned a few things about pruning that seem applicable. The objective of pruning is to produce strong, healthy plants (or in our case, strong, healthy individuals). It is also important to keep pruning tools sharp and in good working condition. Another principle of pruning requires that it be done regularly.

Although some pruning can only be accomplished by the Master Gardener, there are many areas of our lives in which we must take the responsibility for our own pruning. In our lives, *priorities* become our tools for pruning—the tools we must keep sharp and constantly in repair as we determine what we need to cut out from our lives and what we need to leave so that we will become strong and healthy.

In my own life, I can see many things that need to be pruned. Although morning prayer is a priority for me, one day I recognized that I had gotten in the habit of getting up in the morning and turning on the computer to see if I had received any e-mails. Often, after I read the e-mails, something else on the computer would catch my eye, usually something I had no intention of reading. That would lead me to other interesting sites and soon I would be pushed for time, rushing to get dressed and leave for an appointment, never once giving any thought to prayer. One day it hit me: Was it more important for me to check my e-mail than to check in with my Heavenly Father?

Morning prayer was and is one of my highest priorities. What had happened? It was something that happens to all of us from time to time. I had unconsciously let myself slip into a bad habit. I had allowed myself to let something of comparatively little importance take the place of something of critical importance.

It wasn't that I read or looked at anything inappropriate on the computer. It was simply that I became distracted from my priority, from something that I valued, something that I knew made a real difference in how the rest of my day went. It seemed to have happened so gradually that I was totally unaware of the change. Once I recognized this pattern, however, I knew I needed to do some pruning immediately! Like President Brown, I knelt by my bed in prayer, seeking forgiveness and asking for strength from the Master Gardener to live with increased integrity.

As I once again got into the habit of morning prayer, I became increasingly sensitive to how much time I spent at the computer every day. Many times I wasn't really looking for anything specific but was fascinated by how much I could find on a subject. Often I would pursue something that was interesting but certainly not important. Usually I did this when I was preparing a Sunday School lesson. I read far more than was needed or could possibly be used in a lesson. Elder Dallin H. Oaks warned us of such things:

"Temporal circumstances change, but the eternal laws and principles that should guide our choices never change. . . . Because of modern technology, the contents of huge libraries and other data resources are at the fingertips of many of us. Some choose to spend countless hours in unfocused surfing the Internet, watching trivial television, or scanning other avalanches of information. But *to what purpose?*"[3]

These eternal laws and principles should be our priorities—our tools for pruning. After reading and pondering Elder Oaks's statement, I found that the question "To what purpose?" continued to be in my thoughts. I am becoming aware of how many things I do mindlessly. For example, when the mail arrives containing some of my favorite catalogs, I can hardly wait to sit down and look at them. One day, I realized I spent a lot of time looking at catalogs even when there was nothing I needed to purchase! I realized that the ads are attractive and enticing; they accomplish the very purpose for which billions of dollars are spent each year: to convince me to buy something I don't need! I realized anew that here is another area of my life in which I am not living with integrity. Not only was I spending time looking at the catalogs but I was also collecting them in case I might want to make a purchase. One day I took a deep breath and threw away every catalog—the ones stacked for relaxing reading, the ones in the bulging wicker basket in the den, and the ones I had slid under the bed for safekeeping.

ARE THE THINGS THAT KEEP YOU BUSY TAKING YOU WHERE YOU WANT TO GO?

New Era *poster*

I had mixed emotions at first, but when I finished, I

felt wonderful! I did it! It is probably a small thing for others, but for me it was a real victory. Several days after I told this story at a Deseret Book Time Out for Women, I received an e-mail from one of the participants. She told of going home and "attacking" her piles of catalogs. One by one she threw them in the garbage bin, saying, "This one's for me. This one's for Carolyn." If that helps you, great. Just know I don't need any more catalogs!

Please don't get the idea that I think looking at catalogs is wrong or that we should not do it. I am only suggesting that if such an activity prevents us from accomplishing our priorities, we should reexamine how our actions match our beliefs. For example, if I say I have no time to read the scriptures but I spend thirty minutes a day looking at catalogs (or window shopping in the mall, or watching a TV program just because it is on), it would be good for me to examine my priorities and prune away the things that keep me from accomplishing the things that really matter.

"To what purpose?" is a question that will have very different answers for each of us because we are in different stages, ages, and circumstances. How do we determine our priorities? Our Church leaders have given many guidelines that can help us with an activity I call pruning by priorities.

Elder Richard G. Scott taught: "Some places are sacred

and holy where it seems easier to discern the direction of the Holy Spirit. The temple is such a place. Find a retreat of peace and quiet where periodically you can ponder and let the Lord establish the direction of your life. Each of us needs to periodically check our bearings and confirm that we are on course. Sometime soon you may benefit from taking this personal inventory:

"What are my highest priorities to be accomplished while on earth?

"How do I use my discretionary time? Is some of it consistently applied to my highest priorities?

"Is there anything I know I should not be doing? If so, I will repent and stop it now.

"In a quiet moment write down your responses. Analyze them. Make any necessary adjustments.

"Put first things first."[4]

Remember our discussion about repentance? To repent means to have a "change of mind," "a turning of the heart and will to God."[5] When we think of

> ONE OF THE WAYS SATAN LESSENS YOUR EFFECTIVENESS AND WEAKENS YOUR SPIRITUAL STRENGTH IS BY ENCOURAGING YOU TO SPEND LARGE BLOCKS OF YOUR TIME DOING THINGS THAT MATTER VERY LITTLE.
>
> *Elder M. Russell Ballard*

repentance only in relation to having done something wrong, we fail to recognize the importance and power of this principle. We need to *change* the way in which we are doing things so that we might be more in tune spiritually. Then, seeking repentance will help us to turn our hearts to God.

Elder M. Russell Ballard taught: "One of the ways Satan lessens your effectiveness and weakens your spiritual strength is by encouraging you to spend large blocks of your time doing things that matter very little. I speak of such things as sitting for hours on end watching television or videos, playing video games night in and night out, surfing the Internet, or devoting huge blocks of time to sports, games, or other recreational activities.

"Don't misunderstand me," Elder Ballard clarified. "These activities are not wrong in and of themselves (unless, of course, you are watching salacious programs or seeking out pornographic images on the Internet). . . .

"But I speak of letting things get out of balance. . . . One devastating effect of idling away our time is that it deflects us from focusing on the things that matter most. Too many people are willing to sit back and let life just happen to them."[6]

In a talk entitled "Focus and Priorities," Elder Dallin H. Oaks explained that in our day many of us have increased life expectancies, modern timesaving devices, and "far more discretionary time than our predecessors." I was sobered by his next statement: "We are accountable for how we use that time." Elder Oaks then quoted two scriptures: "Thou shalt not idle away thy time" (D&C 60:13) and a commandment given to the early missionaries and members, "Cease to be idle" (D&C 88:124). He continued, "We must begin with focus or we are likely to become like those in the well-known prophecy about people in the last days—'ever learning, and never able to come to the knowledge of the truth' (2 Tim. 3:7)." Then, reminding us of the need for "stillness" in our lives, Elder Oaks taught, "We also need quiet time and prayerful pondering as we seek to develop information into knowledge and mature knowledge into wisdom." He concluded by saying, "Our priorities determine what we seek in life. . . . Our priorities are most visible in how we use our time."[7]

> OUR PRIORITIES DETERMINE WHAT WE SEEK IN LIFE.
>
> Elder Dallin H. Oaks

But how easy it is to lose our focus! I remember visiting a ward in which a woman bore testimony of the power she felt from weekly temple attendance. I stopped listening to what she said because I was having difficulty getting to the temple once a month. How did she manage to go every week? I began making all kinds of assumptions: She must not have very much to do if she can go that often; I bet she doesn't have a very demanding Church calling; she must be wealthy—probably has someone who cleans her house and does her yard. I made one assumption after another, prejudging someone I didn't even know. I was pulled back to her words by the power of the Spirit. I don't know what else she said, but I knew that the Spirit was speaking *to me* and that *I* needed to *make* time to go to the temple.

I usually review my monthly calendar on fast Sunday. After listening to this woman's testimony of the power of weekly temple attendance, I decided to look at my schedule a little more carefully. It was filled with work, preparation for teaching, the usual Church meetings, family commitments, a community play, Relief Society presidency meeting and visiting sisters, a dinner with friends, a dentist appointment, family history I worked on when I could, and other things that just came up. I also knew there were the regular things—cleaning the house, mowing the yard, weeding, washing clothes, grocery shopping, and meal preparation. I felt I deserved some time just for me. There was no way I could go to the temple that coming month! How did this unknown woman manage to go to the temple weekly? She certainly didn't have a schedule like mine!

Then one Sunday during a Relief Society lesson on the importance of the temple in our lives, I sensed once again the prompting of the Spirit: "Make the temple a priority. Schedule it first and fit other obligations around it." It sounded too simple, but the prompting was so strong I decided to try it. I set a specific day and time. I promised myself I would not let anything interfere with that time. Did it work? You bet it did. But *I* had to make temple attendance a priority, rather than hoping I would find a time when I could fit it in.

I remember a colleague with whom I taught at the Orem Institute of Religion. One day, it happened that we were sitting beside each other while waiting for our faculty meeting to begin. His daily planner was open, and I just happened to glance at his "to do" list. The first two items were (1) scripture study and (2) exercise. After the meeting, I asked him, "Why do you put those two items on your 'to do' list? Don't you just do them?"

He quickly flipped through the daily pages of his planner. Every day these two item were listed, and they were always numbers 1 and 2. "If I don't write them down and make a conscious effort to do these things, it is too easy to let something else crowd in." What a lesson for me! Like my colleague and many others, I have a daily "to do" list, but I've never thought of putting things like "scripture study" or "exercise" on the list.

I'll never forget my friend's next statement: "These are two of my highest priorities. Why wouldn't they be on my list?"

For me, making "to do" lists is useful. I love the feeling of satisfaction I get when I check things off. Such lists also help me feel like I'm in control. But I am becoming increasingly aware that this list needs to represent my priorities and not just things that need doing. Just as we make sure our tools are sharp and in good condition before doing any pruning in the yard, so we must make sure our priorities (our tools for pruning our lives) are well established.

As you set about in your own life to "prune by priorities," please consider this counsel from Elder M. Russell Ballard:

"Think about your life and set your priorities. Find some quiet time regularly to think deeply about where you are going and what you will need to do to get there. Jesus, our exemplar, often 'withdrew himself into the wilderness and prayed' (Luke 5:16).

"We need to do the same thing occasionally to rejuvenate ourselves spiritually as the Savior did. Write down the tasks you would like to accomplish each day. Keep foremost in mind the sacred covenants you have made with the Lord as you write down your daily schedules."[8]

GETTING STARTED

1. Take personal inventory as suggested by Elder Scott (see pages 72–73).

2. Make a quiet place and time when you can identify how you have used your discretionary time during the past week. Is some of it applied to your highest priorities?

3. What is *one* change you could make in your life to put first things first?

Scriptures and Thoughts to Ponder

Elder Joseph B. Wirthlin: "That we may do a lot may not be so important. That we focus the energy of our minds, our hearts, and our souls on those things of eternal significance—that is essential."[9]

————————————

Elder William R. Bradford: "Many things, in fact most, are interesting, and many are enticing. But some things are important. The limits of time dictate that we must prioritize what we do. The divinely given and heaven-protected gift of agency allows us to determine to what degree we will serve others and allow them to serve us. The depth of involvement in that which is important, rather than just interesting, is our own choice.”[10]

Sister Patricia Holland served for two years as a counselor to Young Women General President Ardeth G. Kapp. After her release from this calling, Sister Holland had the opportunity to spend a week in Israel. She wrote:

> It had been a very difficult and demanding two years for me. Being a good mother with ample time to succeed at that task has always been my first priority, so I had tried to be a full-time mother to a grade-schooler, a high-schooler, and a son preparing for his mission. I had also tried to be a full-time wife to a staggeringly busy university president. And I had to be as much of a full-time counselor in that general presidency as one living fifty miles from the office could be. But in an important period of forming principles and starting programs, I worried that I wasn’t doing enough—and I tried to run a little faster.
>
> Toward the end of my two-year term, my health was going downhill. I was losing weight steadily, and I wasn’t sleeping well. My husband

and children were trying to bandage me together even as I was trying to do the same for them. We were exhausted. And yet, I kept wondering what I might have done to manage it all better. . . . As grateful as my family was for the conclusion of my term of service, I nevertheless felt a loss of association—and, I confess, some loss of identity—with those women that I had come to love so much. Who was I, and where was I in this welter of demands? Should life be as hard as all this? How successful had I been in my several and competing assignments? Or had I muffed them all? The days after my release were about as difficult as the weeks before it. I didn't have any reserve to call on. My tank was on empty, and I wasn't sure there was a filling station anywhere in sight.

It was just a few weeks later that my husband had the assignment in Jerusalem to which I have referred, and the Brethren traveling on the assignment requested that I accompany him. "Come on," he said. "You can recuperate in the Savior's land of living water and bread of life." As weary as I was, I packed my bags, believing—or, at the very least, hoping—that the time there would be a healing respite.

On a pristinely clear and beautifully bright day, I sat overlooking the Sea of Galilee and reread the tenth chapter of Luke. But instead of the words on the page, I thought I saw with my mind and heard with my heart these words: "[Pat, Pat, Pat], thou art careful and troubled about many things." Then the power of pure and personal revelation seized me as I read, "But one thing [only one thing] is [truly] needful." (Luke 10:40–41.)

The May sun in Israel is so bright you feel as if you are sitting on top of the world. I had just visited the spot in Bethoron where the sun stood still for Joshua (see Josh. 10:12), and indeed, on that day, it seemed so for me as well. As I sat pondering my problems I felt that same sun's healing rays like warm liquid pouring into my heart—relaxing, calming, and comforting my troubled soul.

Our loving Father in Heaven seemed to be whispering to me, "You don't have to worry over so many things. The one thing that is needful—the *only* thing that is truly needful—is to keep your eyes toward the sun—my Son." Suddenly I had true peace. I knew that my life had always been in his hands—from the very beginning! The sea lying peacefully before my eyes had been tempest-tossed and dangerous—many, many times. All I needed to do was to renew my faith, and get a firm grasp on his hand—and *together* we could walk on the water."[11]

Do you ever feel like you're on a treadmill, running as fast as you can but getting nowhere? Then is a good time to stop and ask, "Are the things that keep you busy taking you where you want to go?" (see Matthew 6:33).[12]

Elder Richard G. Scott: "Are there so many fascinating, exciting things to do or so many challenges pressing down upon you that it is hard to keep focused on that which is essential? When things of the world crowd in, all too often the wrong things take highest priority. Then it is easy to forget the fundamental purpose of life. Satan has a powerful tool to use against good people. It is distraction. He would have good people fill life with the 'good things' so there is no room for the essential ones. Have you unconsciously been caught in that trap?"[13]

Seek not to be cumbered.

—Doctrine and Covenants 66:10

let go

six

I was so excited when I found the scripture passage "Seek not to be cumbered" because the only time I remembered ever hearing *cumbered* used was in reference to Martha (Luke 10:40). As I shared my excitement with a friend, she asked, "What exactly does *cumbered* mean?"

"Well," I began with hesitation, "I think I know, but I'd better check the dictionary, just to be sure." We both marveled and were surprised as I read the definitions from Webster's 1828 dictionary. The verb *to cumber* was defined as follows: "to load; to crowd; to check, stop or retard, as by a load or weight; to make motion difficult; to obstruct; to perplex or embarrass; to distract or trouble; to be troublesome to; to cause trouble or obstruction in, as anything useless."[1]

Needless to say, we were both surprised, and we began talking about how so many of the definitions applied to simpli-

CUMBERED: TO LOAD; TO CROWD; TO CHECK, STOP OR RETARD, AS BY A LOAD OR WEIGHT; TO MAKE MOTION DIFFICULT; TO OBSTRUCT; TO PERPLEX OR EMBARRASS; TO DISTRACT OR TROUBLE; TO BE TROUBLESOME TO; TO CAUSE TROUBLE OR OBSTRUCTION IN, AS ANYTHING USELESS.

fying our lives and caring for the life of our souls. We now saw *cumber* in a much broader way than we originally had considered. As you read and ponder this chapter, I invite you to review the definition from time to time, especially as you think of things, attitudes, feelings, thoughts, past deeds, and current habits that cumber you, things of which you might *let go* as you seek to simplify your life.

My first experience with letting go occurred when I was about seven years old. I wanted a two-wheeled bicycle for Christmas so much I could almost taste it! I was just at that age when we had lengthy discussions about whether or not Santa Claus was for real. I didn't take any chances. I wrote Santa a letter explaining how much I needed a bicycle and how I would be able to run errands for Mother. Then, just in case there wasn't a Santa, I made sure Mother and Dad knew how badly I "needed" a bike. Time and time again, both Mother and Dad reminded me, "These are war years; money is tight. Don't get your hopes up for something that you know isn't possible."

But I hoped and I prayed, and on that special Christmas morning, there beside the Christmas tree was a two-wheeled bicycle! I could hardly believe my eyes! It was bright red and shiny beyond belief. I was sure there was a Santa Claus. It would be a long time before I learned how hard my dad had worked to get the dents out of a used bicycle and then paint it my favorite color.

Of course, I begged to go outside and ride it—right then! "Carolyn," Dad said, "there's nearly a foot of snow on the sidewalks."

"But I want to try out my new bike!" Mother convinced me to wait until after all the presents had been opened, and we had finished our traditional Christmas dinner. Then Dad, who was the superintendent of schools and had lots of keys, promised that we would go down to the high school gym and I could ride my new bicycle.

This took place long before the invention of training wheels. In my day, you learned to ride a two-wheeled bicycle by having someone hold you up. Dad had a firm grasp on the back of the seat, and his other hand was right beside mine on the handlebar grip. I could feel myself struggling to stay upright, but Dad held me steady. Around and around the gym we went. Sometimes I felt like Dad was going to let go and I would fall, but he held on tightly.

Then, all of sudden I had it—I felt myself balancing the bicycle all by myself. Dad's steady grip, which I had initially needed so desperately, was now holding me back. I yelled just two words, but I really meant them, "Let go!" I knew I could go faster all by myself. Of course, I wiggled a lot and had my share of falls, but when I could get my balance exactly right, I went so fast I felt like I was flying!

It's a tricky thing—letting go. I would have fallen immediately if Dad had let go the first few times around the gym. But if he had held on forever, I would never have been able to go any faster than he was able to jog alongside me.

Life is much like that. There is a time to hold on and a time to let go. Part of becoming a spiritually mature and responsible adult is learning to differentiate between the times when we should hold on and the times when we need to let go—the things to hold onto and the things to let go of.

Let's look first at things we might consider letting go of. For a long time, I held onto a wool sock I'd purchased in New Zealand. Notice I said "sock." Unfortunately, while on a trip I had lost one of the socks, but I couldn't bring myself to part with the remaining one because it was filled with memories and was one of the finest socks I'd ever had. But every time I put something away in the drawer that held that sock, I'd think, "How silly to hold onto this. Let it go!" I finally did.

But there are so many other, equally strange things I hold on to. For example, I'm becoming aware of how many clothes I have that I haven't worn for years but want to keep just in case I might need them. Finally, I made a rule for myself: If I haven't worn it in the last two years, I give it away! I'm also trying to give something away each time I get something new. I'm still struggling with this, but I am making progress.

Do you keep files of lessons you've taught or articles you like? Pictures you've laminated but haven't used in years? I recently cleaned out a file cabinet that had all of the materials I used to teach institute classes seven years

> PART OF BECOMING A SPIRITUALLY MATURE AND RESPONSIBLE ADULT IS LEARNING TO DIFFERENTIATE BETWEEN THE TIMES WHEN WE SHOULD HOLD ON AND THE TIMES WHEN WE NEED TO LET GO—THE THINGS TO HOLD ONTO AND THE THINGS TO LET GO OF.

ago. I'd never opened one of the drawers in all those years. How valuable could anything be? As I began looking at lessons I'd taught and talks I'd given, I realized that I wouldn't teach the same way today. I'm in a different place spiritually now; I would choose to present the same material differently. "Let go," I told myself as I practically filled a big garbage bin.

On the other hand, I came across materials that I considered historic. It was during the time I served as an assistant to then–BYU presidents Dallin H. Oaks and Jeffrey R. Holland. I had completely forgotten about having attended a meeting on women's issues at which Gloria Steinhem, Betty Freidan, and Bella Abzug (leaders in the women's movement in the 1970s) were the speakers. The file contained not only my notes from that meeting but other things that might have historical significance to someone in the future—pictures, memos to the president, letters to and from general authorities, reports I'd written on the status of women at BYU. I put these things in a box, called the BYU library, and asked if they would be interested in having any of them. Not only was the library pleased that I had offered them these things but I began to realize, in talking with the archivist, that this was indeed an historic time at BYU and in the Church. I realized that some of the women who had been so instrumental in bringing about changes that resulted in the betterment of the status of women had died. I tracked down their daughters, who thankfully had kept their mothers' files and were delighted to learn of a place where they could be appropriately indexed and kept.

Interestingly, most books on the subject of simplifying deal with things—how to organize them, color code the storage of them, and get rid of the many extra things that often clutter our closets and drawers. But I'm convinced that things of a physical nature are the least of what we need to let go.

If we seek to simplify our lives and care for the life of our souls, there are more important things on which we need to focus. What about feelings we harbor? Feelings of envy, anger at something a friend said in a thoughtless moment, variance of opinions, negative attitudes, regret, untrue assumptions, pride, hurt from feeling slighted, anger, or resentment? All of these are negative emotions that poison our souls and sap our energy—and of these things we need to let go.

Such negative feelings arise out of the natural man spoken of by King Benjamin. He tells us how we can overcome such "natural man" feelings by "[yielding] to the enticings of the Holy Spirit, and [putting] off the natural man and [becoming] a saint through the atonement of Christ the Lord, and [becoming] as a child, submissive, meek, humble, patient, full of love, willing to submit to all things which the Lord seeth fit to inflict upon him, even as a child doth submit to his father" (Mosiah 3:19). As Elder Neal A. Maxwell taught, "Conversion basically represents the transformation from the 'natural man' to becoming the 'man of Christ' (Mosiah 3:19; Hel. 3:29; see also 2 Cor. 5:17). It is a labor which takes more than an afternoon."[2]

An unnamed sister shared in an *Ensign* article how she felt when a member of her bishopric expressed displeasure from the pulpit about the way she had handled an assignment with the ward youth. Although he did not mention her name, she knew he was referring to her, and she felt publicly chastised. Her confidence was shaken, her anger stirred, and she had a grudge in her heart that continued to fester long after the event. In the weeks that followed, she did much soul-searching. Through that process she recognized, step by step, that she needed to forgive and support her priesthood leaders. That decision, she wrote, "made my heart soar free from the burden of the grudge I had carried for weeks."

Turning to the scriptures, she read of the time when Moroni worried that the Gentiles would mock him because of his weakness in writing. He prayed that the Lord would give the Gentiles charity. Then our patient Savior taught Moroni: "If they have not charity it mattereth not unto thee, thou hast been faithful" (Ether 12:37). She also read John 21, which records that Christ asked Peter three times if he loved Him. Three times Peter assured the Savior he did. Peter was then commanded, "Feed my sheep."

This sister wrote, "I was familiar with that part of the story, but one day I read beyond it to the end of the chapter." After Peter repeated those words, Christ told him that he would die a martyr. Peter looked at John the Beloved and asked, "Lord, and what shall this man do?" Jesus answered him, "If I will that he tarry till I come, what is that to thee? follow thou me" (John 21:21–22).

"Now when I begin to be offended by one of my brothers or sisters," the unnamed author wrote, "I think of the Savior reminding Moroni that he need only be concerned about the level of charity in himself. I can hear the Lord kindly warning Peter concerning his worry about John's assignment rather than his own. I remember what the Spirit taught me . . . and I am reminded where my focus needs to be. Rather than dwell on the faults of others, I need to focus on my own efforts to be Christlike."[3]

There are many whose lives have been crippled by bitterness, hostility, emotional pain, resentment, grief, disappointment, injustice, or misfortune. Let go! Harboring such feelings destroys the soul and complicates our lives. When we carry feelings that fester our souls, we experience intense suffering and we cannot move forward in our lives—we are literally damned, stopped in our progress! At times we may feel that there is something much too painful or too large, something that we cannot overcome or let go of by ourselves. In that kind of situation, it would be appropriate to seek help from your bishop or a professional counselor. This is especially true when an individual has suffered from some kind of abuse.

Elder Boyd K. Packer once spoke to all who experience feelings of regret, bitterness, grief, and resentment. He told of a saintly man who was steady, serene, and deeply spiritual. His life was one of service to the Church and to the community. As he grew older, he was no longer able to drive at night, and so Elder Packer offered to drive him:

> On one occasion, when the Spirit was right, he gave me a lesson for my life from an experience in his own. Although I thought I had known him, he told me things about his life I would not have supposed.
>
> He grew up in a little community with a desire to make something of himself. He struggled to get an education.
>
> He married his sweetheart, and presently everything was just right. He was well employed,

with a bright future. They were deeply in love, and she was expecting their first child.

The night the baby was to be born, there were complications. The only doctor was somewhere in the countryside tending to the sick.

After many hours of labor, the condition of the mother-to-be became desperate.

Finally the doctor was located. In the emergency, he acted quickly and soon had things in order. The baby was born and the crisis, it appeared, was over.

Some days later, the young mother died from the very infection that the doctor had been treating at another home that night.

John's world was shattered. Everything was not right now; everything was all wrong. He had lost his wife. He had no way to tend both the baby and his work.

As the weeks wore on, his grief festered. "That doctor should not be allowed to practice," he would say. "He brought that infection to my wife. If he had been careful, she would be alive today."

He thought of little else, and in his bitterness, he became threatening. Today, no doubt, he would have been pressed by many others to file a malpractice suit. And there are lawyers who would see in his pitiable condition only one ingredient—money!

But that was another day, and one night a knock came at his door. A little girl said simply, "Daddy wants you to come over. He wants to talk to you."

"Daddy" was the stake president. A grieving, heartbroken young man went to see his spiritual leader.

This spiritual shepherd had been watching his flock and had something to say to him.

The counsel from that wise servant was simply, "*John, leave it alone.* Nothing you do about it will bring her back. Anything you do will make it worse. *John, leave it alone.*"

My friend told me then that this had been his trial—his Gethsemane. How could he leave it alone? Right was right! A terrible wrong had been committed and somebody must pay for it. It was a clear case.

But he struggled in agony to get hold of

himself. And finally, he determined that whatever else the issues were, he should be obedient.

Obedience is powerful spiritual medicine. It comes close to being a cure-all.

He determined to follow the counsel of that wise spiritual leader. He would leave it alone.

Then he told me, "I was an old man before I understood! It was not until I was an old man that I could finally see a poor country doctor—overworked, underpaid, run ragged from patient to patient, with little medicine, no hospital, few instruments, struggling to save lives, and succeeding for the most part.

"He had come in a moment of crisis, when two lives hung in the balance, and had acted without delay.

"I was an old man," he repeated, "before I finally understood! I would have ruined my life," he said, "and the lives of others."

Many times he had thanked the Lord on his knees for a wise spiritual leader who counseled simply, *"John, leave it alone."*

Elder Packer concluded: "Purge and cleanse and soothe your soul and your heart and your mind and that of others.

"A cloud will then be lifted, a beam cast from your eye. There will come that peace which surpasseth understanding."[4]

I believe there are times when we are not even aware of resentments or anger that we carry in our hearts, feelings that are destructive to ourselves and to our relationships with others. You might have noticed that nearly every personal experience in this book is about me and my father. Have you wondered where my mother was when I was growing up? I was raised as an only child until I was ten and a half. Then, my mother gave birth to my brother, Mark. She was forty-five years of age at the time, and though I understood little of what was really happening (such things were not discussed in the 1940s), I now realize she suffered a severe case of postpartum depression. She was told to stay in bed, and I was told to take care of my brother. My aunt came to stay with us for two weeks and taught me how to make formula, rinse out diapers in the toilet, wash them and run them through the wringer, and hang them on the line. When Mark cried, I did what I could to attend to him. When my friends were going to the basketball game, I was baby-sitting.

I had never talked about any of this and am not sure that I realized how resentful I felt that I had been displaced by a baby for whom I was always responsible. The one thing I did know was that I was no longer an only child—I was a mother! I always knew my relationship with Mother was strained, but not until the last years of her life was I able to fully understand all that happened.

When Mother was in her nineties and we were talking of old times, she said to me, "Do you know how hurt I felt when Mark was a baby and would cry? I would go to comfort him, but he always wanted to go to you!"

I was shocked. Had Mother felt this way and harbored those feelings for more than fifty years? All of a sudden I saw things from a different perspective. I thought *I* was the one who had been hurt when Mark was born, but it was Mother who had carried this pain for so many years.

That night, I suggested to Mother that I give her a bath. She could not get in or out of the tub without help. I scrubbed her back, washed her feet, and cleaned her fingernails. "Oh, this feels so good" she kept saying. All the while, with each little motion, I found that it was not just her body that was being cleansed—it was *my* heart!

Just before she was ready to get out of the tub, I ran and put the towels in the clothes dryer. When they were warm, I wrapped them around her. I asked if she remembered how she would place the towels on the radiator when I was a little girl and then when I got out of the tub, wrap them around me. We both remembered with fondness.

I helped Mother sit on the toilet so I could dry her feet. Tears ran down my face, and when I looked up, I saw that she, too, was crying. "You shouldn't have to do this for me. I'm your mother," she insisted.

"But you did it for me. Now it's my turn," I responded.

As our tears mingled together, our hearts were mended as well. We both let go of feelings that had stifled our relationship for many years. That night as we prayed together, I knew we had been healed by the mercy of Jesus Christ, the Balm of Gilead—a balm symbolic for its power to soothe and heal.

> *There is a balm in Gilead*
> *To make the wounded whole*
> *There is a balm in Gilead*
> *To heal the sin-sick soul.*[5]

I am acquainted with so many good and righteous women who question and wonder who they really are and who harbor feelings of inadequacy and worthlessness. They think they are not thin enough, pretty enough, talented enough, smart enough, and so forth. When I hear these comments I want to yell out, ENOUGH! LET GO! You are enough—just the way you are. You are a spirit daughter of Heavenly Parents.

Just as your physical body resembles those of the earthly parents who created it, so you have a spirit body created by your Heavenly Parents! Your spirit looks like and is like theirs. You have inherited divine, godlike qualities that you need to develop. You are of infinite worth. You have your own divine potential.

Holding on to true doctrine is critical. One of my favorite quotations is from President George Q. Cannon, who served as a counselor to four presidents of the Church. In a compilation of his writings is this powerful statement: "God in His infinite mercy has revealed to us a great truth. It is a truth that, when understood by us, gives a new light to our existence and inspires us with the most exalted hopes. *That truth is that God is our Father, and we are His children*. . . . Is this literally true? The answer is, 'Yes.' God has revealed it, that we are literally His children, His offspring, that we are just as much His children as our offspring are our children, that He begot us, and that we existed with Him in the family relationship as His children."[6]

This is one of those doctrines that *if* we accept and act upon it, it will change our lives. As Elder Boyd K. Packer has taught: "True doctrine, understood, changes attitudes and behavior. The study of the doctrines of the gospel will improve behavior quicker than a study of behavior will improve behavior. Preoccupation with unworthy behavior can lead to unworthy behavior. That is why we stress so forcefully the study of the doctrines of the gospel."[7]

The messages of the world are something of which we need to let go if we are serious about caring for the life of our souls. For example, unless we understand and accept the doctrine that we are literal children of God, the messages of the world will confuse us and confound us. Billions of dollars are paid to advertising agencies to convince us that we need what they are selling if we are to be of worth. Recently I read an ad that said, "Clothes make the woman. Clothes hide who you aren't." This is Satan's way of trying to confuse us. True doctrine, understood and held onto, will give us the strength to let go of the falsehoods of the world.

Nancy M. Christensen shared in an *Ensign* article that all of her life she had been worried about "what if?" Her "what ifs" ranged from wondering if she would be chosen for a team in school to wondering if she was good enough. As she grew to adulthood she continued to have even more plaguing questions that resulted in anxiety attacks. She wondered what she could do or where she might find relief as her "what ifs" multiplied into thoughts of not wanting to be left alone or to drive a car. She became even more anxious when she realized such feelings were not "reasonable expectations for a mother of four young children."

Her answer came one fast Sunday. These questions had weighed heavily on her mind. As soon as the meetings were over, her five- and seven-year-old sons raced to see who could get home first. They each grabbed the door handle, trying to turn the knob of the locked door. When the mother arrived home, she put the key in the lock, but because of the boys' strong grip, she could not turn the key. Out of her mouth tumbled the words, "If you would just let go for a minute, I could turn the key and let you in."

Then she shared her "personal parable for peace": "As I said those words, an image popped into my mind. I imagined the Savior standing next to me, repeating my own words back to me: 'If you would just let go for a minute, I could turn the key for you. Let go. Let me help.'

"I had my answer," she wrote. "I realized that by letting go of the fear and worry, I could open myself up to the love of the Savior. My fears may or may not materialize, but when I trust in the Lord, somehow things work out for the best.

"As I let go of my worries and put my trust in the Savior, I have gained a testimony that through the Atonement, our most difficult burdens can be lifted."[8]

It is likely, as you have read this chapter, that things

came to your mind, things you need to let go. But I know from my own experience that sometimes the things we most need to let go of, we hold onto the tightest. That reminds me of the monkey trap made from a hollowed-out coconut into which has been placed a nut. The hole is large enough for the monkey to insert his hand, but once he has hold of the nut, his fist is too big to go through the hole.

OF THOSE THINGS THAT WOULD CANKER AND FESTER YOUR SOUL—*LET GO.* OF THE TRUE DOCTRINE THAT CAN CHANGE OUR ATTITUDES AND BEHAVIOR—*HOLD ON* WITH ALL YOUR MIGHT!

Sometimes the burdensome things of the heart are easily identified. At other times we hold on to "nuts" without really realizing that they complicate our lives and eat away at our souls. Often, we need Christ's wisdom and strength to help us identify those things we need to let go of and to teach us the things that are of such worth that we need to hang onto them with all of our strength.

Each of us so desperately needs the Balm of Gilead in our lives—that healing that comes from letting go of sin, offenses, resentments, and anger; sometimes we need to forgive ourselves. Likewise, we have need to cleanse and purge our souls, hearts, and minds. Such cleansing and purging bring about healing—a healing of our souls. Of those things that would canker and fester your soul—*let go.* Of the true doctrine that can change our attitudes and behavior—*hold on* with all your might!

GETTING STARTED

1. Think of one thing you could let go of. I like to start in the smallest room first—the bathroom. Do you have a hair product that's just sitting on a shelf—one you bought several years ago because your hair stylist told you it would be the perfect thing for your hair? If you don't like it and never use it— LET GO!

2. Are you like me with the catalogs? If so, take a deep breath and LET GO.

3. Find a quiet place and time, even if it means going without lunch one day, to ask Heavenly Father to help you honestly examine your heart, to make it pure before Him. Are you carrying burdens that weigh you down? Are you carrying resentment, envy, pride, guilt, remorse, or other ill feelings? Listen to the whisperings of the Holy Ghost. Ask Heavenly Father to help you know how to eliminate these feelings and move forward.

Scriptures and Thoughts to Ponder

Read Alma 5:14–31. Think of this passage as a "self-evaluation interview" with Alma. Be mindful of the things that the people of Zarahemla were counseled to hold on to and the things they were to let go of. Conclude by reading Alma 5:33–35. Read the verses as if Alma were speaking directly to you.

Elder Boyd K. Packer: "If you resent someone for something he [or she] has done—or failed to do—forget it.

"Too often the things we carry are petty, even stupid. If you are still upset after all these years that Aunt Clara didn't come to your wedding reception, why don't you grow up and forget it?

"If you brood constantly over a loss or past mistake, look ahead—settle it.

"We call that forgiveness. Forgiveness is powerful spiritual medicine. To extend forgiveness, that soothing balm, to those who have offended you is to heal. And, more difficult yet, when the need is there, forgive yourself!"[9]

Elder Joseph B. Wirthlin: "Sometimes we feel that the busier we are, the more important we are—as though our busyness defines our worth. . . . We can spend a lifetime whirling about at a feverish pace, checking off list after list of things that in the end really don't matter.

"That we do a lot may not be so important. That we focus the energy of our minds, our hearts, and our souls on those things of eternal significance—that is essential."[10]

Cindy K. Peterson: "Too often I find myself so wrapped up in the thick of thin things that I feel almost as though I can't breathe, let alone rest. I drain my energy dry doing ten worthwhile activities—and neglect three eternally important ones. At times like this, I could learn from the counsel Moses' father-in-law gave him: 'The thing that thou doest is not good. Thou wilt surely wear away . . . for this thing is too heavy for thee; thou art not able to perform it.' (Ex. 18:17–18.) Several weeks ago I looked back over my daily schedules and realized I had wasted much energy and had worn myself out over things that were overdone or were in some ways unnecessary. So what if I baked several varieties of cookies for the party and found the best buys in town if I'm too tired to cuddle with my children or be with my husband or if I fall asleep while I'm trying to say my prayers?"[11]

*With God nothing shall
be impossible.*

—Luke 1:37

Not long ago, I experienced one of those days when I had had it. My schedule was packed from morning until evening, I had classes for which I needed to prepare, talks to write, Church responsibilities to complete, a lawn that needed mowing, and washing that needed to be done. My "to do" list was longer than the paper it was written on and was more than I felt I could accomplish. I got in my car, drove to a side road, and yelled, "Stop the world! I want to get off!"

Having released a little bit of built-up stress, I began churning inside. I thought, "I can't go on like this. I can't do everything I'm supposed to do. I'm not doing anything well. I feel like I'm going to explode!"

I arrived home to an answering machine that had more

messages than I wanted to listen to, and nearly every one contained a request.

"Do you have your visiting teaching done for the month?"

"No!" I yelled back to no one.

"Could you substitute for the Gospel Doctrine class on Sunday?"

"No!" I yelled.

"Can you take in a meal to Sister Jones?"

"No! Can't her children do something once in a while?"

Fortunately, my answering machine doesn't record my responses to the people who've called. But I couldn't do one more thing. I was physically exhausted, emotionally drained, and completely devoid of the Spirit.

I have talked with many who experience such feelings of anxiety, frustration, and stress. At times we feel out of control, especially when demands are made upon us by others—family members, Church leaders, the PTA, visiting teaching, home responsibilities, or work obligations. But sometimes, *we* are the guilty ones—we put things on ourselves that stretch us beyond our capacity to bear. When we look at our priorities, we might be doing things that don't need to be done. Do we really have to serve refreshments at *every* meeting? Do cookies *have* to be homemade? Does anyone really care about a handout, or will it simply be thrown away when class members get home? Does a name tag have to be hand colored to be effective? Could a 3x5 card serve the same purpose?

Likewise, we sometimes create unrealistic deadlines for ourselves. Would it make any real difference if you waited until tomorrow to stop at the post office for stamps? Is it possible that a phone call would be just as appreciated as a visit? Could an e-mail or a few phone calls accomplish as much as a face-to-face meeting?

Often I find that I put pressure on myself just because I anticipated doing something on a specific day when it could easily be done later in the week. A friend once pointed out to me that Doctrine and Covenants 88:119 reads: "Organize yourselves; prepare every needful thing." It does *not* read, "Prepare EVERYthing."

This is why "pruning by priorities" becomes so essential. Elder Neal A. Maxwell taught: "Sometimes, unintentionally, even certain extracurricular Church activities, insensitively administered, can hamper family life.

"Instructively, after the resurrected Jesus taught the Nephites, He said, 'Go ye unto your homes, and ponder upon the things which I have said,' and pray and prepare 'for the morrow' (3 Ne. 17:3).

"Jesus did not say go to your civic clubs, town meetings, or even stake centers!"[1]

Similarly, Elder Richard G. Scott counseled, "May I give you a word of caution as you plan your activities. Make sure that the essential needs are met, but do not go overboard in creating so many good things to do that the essential ones are not accomplished. . . . Remember, don't magnify the work to be done—simplify it."[2] While Elder Scott was speaking specifically about Church activities, I believe the same principle applies to every aspect of our lives.

The bottom line is that it is impossible to do everything, be everything, and meet everyone's expectations. That is an important lesson to learn. And if you're like me, it is a lesson to be reminded of again and again.

There is another aspect associated with *impossible*. There have been many times in my life when I've felt overwhelmed, uptight, and totally stressed. Remember the statement "Stress drives away the Spirit"? I experience that more often than I'd like to admit. I think it is not an uncommon feeling, especially among women. We have a tendency to believe that we have to do everything all by ourselves. Nothing could be further from the truth! I'm not talking about calling in the Relief Society or even your visiting teacher. I'm talking about calling on a *heavenly power*—a power promised us by the Savior.

This power is known as grace. The Bible Dictionary explains, "The main idea of the word [*grace*] is divine means of help or strength, given through the bounteous mercy and love of Jesus Christ."[3] Through Christ's bounteous love and mercy, we have access to "divine means of help or strength"—literally, an "enabling power."

I'll use the writing of this book as an example. I have to admit there were times when I thought I knew exactly what I wanted to write, but no matter how much I thought about it, I simply could not find a way to convey my thoughts in writing. When that happened, I would kneel in prayer, acknowledging that I could not write this book without Heavenly Father's help. Many, many times, thoughts and words would come into my mind, ideas far better than anything I had thought of. I soon learned that it was critical for me to begin my writing sessions with prayer. In some instances, stories came to mind that I'd not thought of in years; in other instances, I would remember a specific talk by a General Authority or a scripture. I knew I was experiencing His enabling power and that I was being enabled to write beyond my natural abilities.

Elder David A. Bednar, while serving as a member of the Seventy and president of BYU–Idaho before his call to the Quorum of the Twelve, said, "I suspect [we] are much more familiar with the nature of the redeeming power of the atonement than we are with the enabling power of the atonement."

He suggested that most of us understand that Christ came to earth to die for us, to pay the price for our sins and to make us clean, to redeem us from our fallen state, and to enable every person to be resurrected from the dead. In other words, we know the Atonement is for sinners. But, Elder Bednar added, "I frankly do not think many of us 'get it' concerning this enabling and strengthening aspect of the atonement, and I wonder if we mistakenly believe we must make the journey from good to better and become a saint all by ourselves, through sheer grit, willpower, and discipline, and with our obviously limited capacities."[4]

> I FRANKLY DO NOT THINK MANY OF US "GET IT" CONCERNING THIS ENABLING AND STRENGTHENING POWER OF THE ATONEMENT.
>
> *Elder David A. Bednar*

I'm the first to admit my own guilt in frequently believing that through "sheer grit, willpower, and discipline" I can manage just about anything. I think this is not an uncommon feeling among many of us. We have a tendency to believe that we have to do everything all by ourselves. I know that nothing is further from the truth; I have repeatedly experienced the enabling power promised by the Savior, but I so easily forget and am so slow to remember.

Recently, as I was studying about the enabling power of the Atonement, I talked with several women who have struggled under very difficult circumstances and who have each prevailed by coming to rely on Christ, who enabled them to carry on when burdens seemed too heavy and pain too intense to bear.

A dear friend lovingly cared for her brilliant husband, who experienced early onset Alzheimer's disease. He also suffered physical illnesses. She was widowed at fifty-five. She told me, "There are times when the sadness is overwhelming. I get on my knees and plead, 'you have to carry this for a while. I can't do this alone.' And I feel His strength; strength enough to allow me to move forward and face each day, one at a time. To me, this is the power of the Atonement. I know He will not change my situation; the only thing I can change is me—I have to humble myself and call on Him for help. Through this experience, I am coming to know the Savior as a person—not just someone I read about in the scriptures, but I am developing a relationship with Him."[5]

I also spoke with a woman I'd become acquainted with in an institute class I taught several years ago. Frequently she would stop by my office after class. Over many months, she shared bits of her life story. She had suffered a variety of kinds of abuse. I will forever remember the day she came to my office pleading for help. I sensed her pain, but I have no training in how to handle such things, and I pleaded with the Lord to know how I might help. I played Church hymns and continued to pray silently. After a very long time, when I sensed she had calmed down, I invited her to sit in my office chair. On the wall, at eye level, was a painting of Christ. I invited her to look into His eyes as I began reading from the scriptures.

"Fear not, little flock. . . . Look unto me in every thought; doubt not, fear not" (D&C 6:34–36).

The Lord has said: "For can a woman forget her sucking child, that she should not have compassion on the son of her womb? Yea, they may forget, yet will I not forget thee. . . . Behold, I have graven thee upon the palms of my hands" (1 Nephi 21:15–16).

Christ "shall go forth, suffering pains and afflictions and temptations of every kind; and this that the word might be fulfilled which saith he will take upon him the pains and the sicknesses of his people . . . and he will take upon him their infirmities, that his bowels may be filled with mercy, according to the flesh, that he may know according to the flesh how to succor his people according to their infirmities" (Alma 7:11–12).

"Look unto God . . . and pray unto him with exceeding faith, and he will console you in your afflictions, and he will plead your cause. . . . O all ye that are pure in heart, lift up your heads and receive the pleasing word of God, and feast upon his love" (Jacob 3:1–2).

Without question, I knew I had been blessed by the love and mercy of Jesus Christ to do and say things beyond my natural ability. For my friend, it was a new beginning. At my request she wrote how she remembered that day:

"I felt an overwhelming feeling of love and peace. Intellectually, I knew about the Atonement, but that day I came to 'heart knowledge' as I *felt* His healing power. I came to know that ultimately true healing can only come from the Master Physician, Jesus Christ."[6]

I also became acquainted with a young mother with two active boys under the age of three. Her husband is in college and works two jobs. Both hold responsible callings in the ward. I don't remember ever seeing her without a smile on her face and a warm greeting for everyone. You can imagine my surprise when I learned that she suffers from the painful and debilitating disease of rheumatoid arthritis. "How do you manage?" I asked her.

"Well," she hesitated, "I'm learning to submit to His will, especially when every joint aches and I only have energy enough to lie on the couch and watch the boys play."

"But you never miss church and are always so pleasant," I said. "How do you do it?"

I was not prepared for the simplicity of her answer. "We try to do what we are asked—to hold family home evening, read the scriptures every day, and pray. I am so grateful for prayer. Several months ago I wanted so badly to have a party for my son's first birthday. I prayed to Heavenly Father, 'You know how to help me. This isn't for me; it's for my son.' When I finished that prayer, I knew I would be sustained."[7]

I think of so many I know who have not yet come to believe all that Christ promises. If you are in need of His grace, that divine means of strength and help, to deal with the stresses and challenges in your life, will you accept Christ's invitation? "Peace I leave with you," He says, "my peace I give unto you. . . . Let not your heart be troubled, neither let it be afraid" (John 14:27).

Of this invitation, Elder Jeffrey R. Holland made this thought-provoking statement: "I submit to you, that may be one of the Savior's commandments that is, even in the hearts of otherwise faithful Latter-day Saints, almost universally disobeyed; and yet I wonder whether our resistance to this invitation could be any more grievous to the Lord's merciful heart." He added, "In [this] same spirit I am convinced that none of us can appreciate how deeply it wounds the loving heart of the

Savior of the world when he finds that his people do not feel confident in his care or secure in his hands."[8]

Do we fully understand how sincere the Savior is when He offers to help us? He stands ever ready to strengthen us and calm us, to help us distinguish the important and essential things from those that make little difference. But we must come unto Him to receive His gift of grace.

Moroni records the words which the Lord spoke to him when he was worried that others, in years to come, would ridicule the way he had recorded the testimony of his people: "Fools mock, but they shall mourn; and *my grace* is sufficient for the meek, that they shall take no advantage of your weakness; and if men come unto me I will show unto them their weakness. I give unto men weakness that they may be humble; and my *grace* [my enabling power] is sufficient for all men that humble themselves before me; for if they humble themselves before me, and have faith in me, *then will I make weak things become strong unto them*" (Ether 12:26–27; emphasis added).

These scriptures suggest that part of the reason we experience "weakness" is so we can learn to acknowledge that we do indeed need strength beyond our own. Our weaknesses turn us to Jesus Christ. It is through our faith in Him and His mercy and love for us that we come to know there is divine help available to each of us. The Apostle Paul must have understood this well, for he wrote in his letter to the Philippians, "I can do all things through Christ which strengtheneth me" (Philippians 4:13). Likewise, Ammon, when his brother Aaron rebuked him because he thought he was boasting, said, "I do not boast in my own strength, nor in my own wisdom. . . . Yea, I know that I am nothing; as to my strength I am weak; therefore I will not boast of myself, but I will boast of my God, for *in his strength I can do all things*" (Alma 26:11–12; emphasis added).

As we consider this divine means of help and strength, we need to recognize that nothing pleases Satan more than for us to think there is no higher source of power available to us, that we are literally alone and have to do everything all by ourselves. The adversary knows that when we understand the enabling power of the Atonement, we will have strength beyond our natural abilities, our weakness will be turned to strength,

IF SATAN CAN PREVENT US FROM LEARNING THE DOCTRINE OF CHRIST'S ATONEMENT AND DRAWING UPON THE ENABLING POWER OF THAT ATONEMENT, HE WILL LEAVE US CRIPPLED, WEAK, AND INEFFECTIVE— "MISERABLE LIKE UNTO HIMSELF" (2 NEPHI 2:27).

and we will know that "in the strength of the Lord [we] canst do all things" (Alma 20:4). Christ has the power to heal our feelings of fear, self-doubt, sorrow, discouragement, and inadequacy. He will help us get through difficult days and trying times if we but come unto Him. If Satan can prevent us from learning the doctrine of Christ's atonement and drawing upon the enabling power of that Atonement, he will leave us crippled, weak, and ineffective—"miserable like unto himself" (2 Nephi 2:27).

When we feel overburdened, discouraged, stressed, and overwhelmed, we need to stop ourselves, not the world. We need to "be still, and know that [He is] God" (Psalm 46:10).

One of my favorite hymns is "Lean on My Ample Arm." It is written as if Christ Himself were speaking to us:

> *Lean on my ample arm,*
> *O thou depressed!*
> *And I will bid the storm*
> *Cease in thy breast.*
> *Whate'er thy lot may be*
> *On life's complaining sea,*
> *If thou wilt come to me,*
> *Thou shalt have rest.*[9]

In the familiar hymn "How Firm a Foundation," we again hear Christ's voice saying,

> *Fear not, I am with thee; oh, be not dismayed,*
> *For I am thy God and will still give thee aid.*
> *I'll strengthen thee, help thee, and cause thee to stand,*
> . . . .
> *Upheld by my righteous, omnipotent hand.*
>
> *When through fiery trials thy pathway shall lie,*
> *My grace, all sufficient, shall be thy supply.*
> *The flame shall not hurt thee; I only design*
> . . . .
> *Thy dross to consume and thy gold to refine.*[10]

Did you notice the statement "My grace, all sufficient, shall be thy supply"? Think again of the Bible Dictionary definition of the word *grace*: "the main idea of the word [grace] is *divine means of help or strength,* given through the bounteous mercy and love of Jesus Christ."[11]

There are many hymns in which the author uses the word *grace*. The next time you sing "Come, Come, Ye Saints," don't think of the history of the hymn or of the pioneers coming across the plains. Instead, think of yourself as you sing, "Though hard to [me] this journey may appear, *Grace* shall be as [my] day."[12] However difficult your situation, your circumstances, your day, you will have enough grace—enough of Christ's enabling power.

How do we begin to allow the Atonement to work in our lives? What do we need to do? It is simpler than most of us think. When we feel stressed, troubled, unsure, or discouraged, we need to remember the things that are taught in Primary: We must believe in Christ and all He has promised to do for us. Obeying His commandments and partaking of the sacrament brings us strength beyond our own. Prayer, fasting, study of the scriptures, and temple worship also bring us close to Him where we can feel His love and His power; power to accomplish whatever faces us in our lives.

> IF YOU EVER BECOME DISCOURAGED OR FEEL TOO WEAK TO CONTINUE LIVING THE GOSPEL, REMEMBER THE STRENGTH YOU CAN RECEIVE THROUGH THE ENABLING POWER OF GRACE.
>
> *True to the Faith*

These are heady thoughts, but true doctrine—doctrine, which if understood, will not only bless our daily lives but help us as we face challenges and days that seem overwhelming if we are left to our own power.

I love this statement from the Church publication *True*

to the Faith: A Gospel Reference: "If you ever become discouraged or feel too weak to continue living the gospel, remember the strength you can receive through the enabling power of grace."[13]

The next time you are faced with a task or a personal challenge that seems *impossible* for you to accomplish or deal with, repeat the following six words: "With God nothing shall be impossible" (Luke 1:37).

GETTING STARTED

1. Think of a time when you felt the enabling power of Christ in your life. Reflect upon that feeling. For most of us, this was not manifest in a large way, but in small, quiet things—perhaps the discovery of a scripture that seemed "just for you," a comment from a branch or ward member that was just what you needed, a thought that came as you sang a hymn or listened to another's testimony.

2. Listen to general conference or read the articles in the *Ensign* or the *Liahona.* Identify some specific things taught by the Brethren concerning grace or the power of Christ manifest in the lives of others.

3. The next time you feel out of control, overwhelmed, discouraged, or inadequate, turn to your scriptures. Read the definition of *grace* in the Bible Dictionary. If you have time,

reread this chapter or some of the scriptures or thoughts listed below.

Scriptures and Thoughts to Ponder

> *Bid thine heart all strife to cease;*
> *With thy brethren be at peace.*
> *Oh, forgive as thou wouldst be*
> *E'en forgiven now by me.*
> *In the solemn faith of prayer*
> *Cast upon me all thy care,*
> *And my Spirit's grace shall be*
> *Like a fountain unto thee.*[14]

Elder Neal A. Maxwell: "Jesus not only took upon Him our sins to atone for them, but also our sicknesses and aching griefs (see Alma 7:11–12; Matt. 8:17). Hence, He knows personally all that we pass through and how to extend His perfect mercy—as well as how to succor us."[15]

Ronald O. Barney: "Mary Ann Brown and her family lived in a one-room dugout for nine years. Six of her 10 children died in infancy or childhood. Yet in the personal history she dictated near the end of her life, she said, 'We endured willingly many hardships and cheerfully made many sacrifices in order to carry on what we sincerely believed to be God's work in subduing a desert and advancing civilization, and in this God acknowledged us and make us feel His approval and His guiding supporting hand.'"[16]

*The Lord will give strength
unto his people; the Lord will
bless his people with peace.*

—Psalm 29:11

fortify

I love words. I like looking them up in various dictionaries, learning their derivations, and learning the root from which a particular word and related words come. The root word of *fortify* is easy to recognize—fort. A fort is a place built to ensure safety to those inside it. Forts were often surrounded by a ditch, rampart, or stockade. However they were constructed, a fort was built for one purpose—security against the enemy. Reformer Martin Luther penned the words, "A mighty *fortress* is our God, / A tower of *strength* ne'er failing."[1]

The word *fort* comes from the Latin word *fortis,* meaning "strong." You may also recognize a related Latin word *fortius* as one of the words from the Olympic motto "Citius, Altius, Fortius," which means "Swifter, Higher, Stronger." *Fortify* differs from the words *fort, fortress,* and *fortius* in that it is a verb—a word of action. To fortify means "to strengthen against attack; to impart strength or endurance to; to strengthen mentally or morally."[2]

TO FORTIFY: TO STRENGTHEN AGAINST ATTACK; TO IMPART STRENGTH OR ENDURANCE TO; TO STRENGTHEN MENTALLY OR MORALLY.

The word *fortify* (in various forms) is used repeatedly throughout Alma 49 and 50. Moroni desired that the Nephite people and their cities be fortified against the attack of their enemies, the Lamanites. In preparation for probable attack from the Lamanites, Moroni "stationed an army by the borders of the city"; he had the people "cast up dirt round about to shield them from the arrows and the stones." The Nephites "had dug up a ridge of earth round about them" that was so high that the stones and arrows of the enemy could not "take effect" (Alma 49:2, 4).

What was the result of this preparation, this effort to fortify themselves and their cities? "The chief captains of the Lamanites were astonished exceedingly, because of the wisdom of the Nephites in preparing their places of security." To the Lamanites' "uttermost astonishment," the Nephites were prepared for them. They retreated because they "knew not that Moroni had fortified, or had built forts of security, for every city in all the land round about" (Alma 49:5, 8, 13).

Because of these fortifications, not a single Nephite was killed. They acknowledged the hand of the Lord in their protection, and perhaps most important, "there was continual peace among them, and exceedingly great prosperity in the church because of their heed and diligence which they gave unto the word of God" (Alma 49:30; see also vv. 23–29). It is impressive to me that they did not stop making preparations after they won the battle but continued to "prepare strongholds" against possible future attacks by the Lamanites (Alma 50:6).

The weapons of war used in Book of Mormon times are not used today, and the enemies that surround us are very different. In truth, there has never been a time in the history of the world when there has been a greater need to fortify ourselves, our families, our homes, and our communities against invasion by multiple enemies. And the enemy is not "out there somewhere." The enemy comes into our homes through the Internet, television, rented or purchased DVDs, MP3 downloads, graphic portrayals on the covers of weekly news magazines, and the many text messages exchanged between youth. We live in a time of increasing immorality, sexual permissiveness, brutality, abuse, violence, natural disasters, pornography, salacious advertising, drugs, war, corruption, and sorrow.

If we are to simplify our lives, we need to focus on the things that will fortify us spiritually. Remember, "many things, in fact most, are interesting, and many are enticing. But some things are important."[3] Fortifying ourselves spiritually against the temptations and challenges of our day is important, if not essential.

President Hinckley has warned: "No one need tell you that we are living in a very difficult season in the history of the world. Standards are dropping everywhere. Nothing seems to be sacred any more. . . .

" . . . The traditional family is under heavy attack. I do not know that things were worse in the times of Sodom and Gomorrah. . . . We see similar conditions today. They prevail all across the world.

" . . . Our Father must weep as He looks down upon His wayward sons and daughters.

"In the Church we are working very hard to stem the tide of this evil. But it is an uphill battle."[4]

Likewise, Elder Boyd K. Packer taught: "These are days of great spiritual danger for this people. The world is spiraling downward at an ever-quickening pace. I am sorry to tell you it will not get better.

"I know of nothing in the history of the Church or in the history of the world to compare with our present circumstances. Nothing happened in Sodom and Gomorrah which exceeds the wickedness and depravity which surrounds us now."[5]

But our living prophets do not sound warnings without giving us counsel—counsel on how we can *fortify* ourselves to live in these challenging times. Elder Dallin H. Oaks taught:

"We need to make both temporal and spiritual preparation for the events prophesied at the time of the Second Coming. And the preparation most likely to be neglected is the one less visible and more difficult—the spiritual. . . . There are many temporal causes of commotion, including wars and natural disasters, but an even greater cause of current 'commotion' is spiritual."[6]

Elder Henry B. Eyring counseled: "As the forces around us increase in intensity, whatever spiritual strength was once sufficient will not be enough. And whatever growth in spiritual strength we once thought was possible, greater growth will be made available to us. Both the need for spiritual strength and the opportunity to acquire it will increase at rates which we underestimate at our peril. . . .

". . . I plead with you to do with determination the simple things that will move you forward spiritually. . . .

". . . You have the right and the obligation to choose for yourselves. You can search the scriptures or not. You can choose to work hard enough, to ponder, and to obey His commandments so that the Holy Ghost can be your companion. . . . Or you can choose to delay. . . .

". . . If you will let your heart be drawn to the Savior and always remember Him, and if you will draw near to our Heavenly Father in prayer, you will have put on spiritual armor. You will be protected."[7]

> DO WITH DETERMINATION
>
> THE SIMPLE THINGS THAT
>
> WILL MOVE YOU FORWARD
>
> SPIRITUALLY.
>
> *Elder Henry B. Eyring*

I invite you to ponder Elder Eyring's counsel to "do with determination the simple things that will move you forward spiritually." Note three things about his teaching:

1. We have "the right and the obligation" to choose for ourselves what we will do.

2. Several "simple things" are suggested that will fortify us spiritually: scripture reading, pondering and obeying the commandments, praying, and remembering Jesus Christ.

3. If we do these things, Elder Eyring promises us, we

will be protected. In other words, we will have *fortified* ourselves spiritually as the evil forces around us increase.

During a very difficult time in my life, I was taught what I must do to fortify myself spiritually. Shortly after I joined the Church in 1971, I faced many challenges. My parents, especially my mother, felt I had abandoned my heritage in the Lutheran Church and all the things I had been taught. Friends who heard about my conversion suggested that I'd been brainwashed, that my Mormon "friends" would have rejected me if I hadn't joined "their" Church. A colleague from an eastern university took me to lunch during a professional conference. It was only weeks after my baptism, and I enthusiastically told her of my conversion and baptism. After hearing my "good news," she asked me many questions about the teachings and doctrine of the Church. I felt I was being interrogated! I was a four-week-old convert and did not have a depth of knowledge of the scriptures nor a comprehensive understanding of the doctrines of the restored gospel. I had made the decision to be baptized because "everything felt so right." As we concluded our lunch, my friend said, "I don't care which church you belong to. But I don't think *you think* you made the right decision in joining the Mormon Church."

I ran back to my hotel room, shaken. My head was spinning. Had I been brainwashed? Had my new friends pressured me into being baptized? Had I made the right decision? Did I really feel the power of the Spirit or was I merely feeling the approval of my Mormon friends? The more I reviewed these thoughts, the more confused I became. I changed my plane reservations and returned to Utah earlier than I had planned. I hoped that being among Church members would bring a reassurance that the decision I had made was right.

For nearly a month, I walked around in a daze, reviewing what led up to my decision to be baptized and questioning the action I had taken. I cried until there were no tears left. I felt exhausted, but sleep seldom came. I was afraid to talk with anyone about my dilemma and intentionally isolated myself, even to the point of not attending sacrament and other meetings. I was sure I would fail the graduate classes I was taking that semester. I gave serious thought to running away, to transferring my credits to another university, and never mentioning to anyone that I was ever a member of The Church of Jesus Christ of Latter-day Saints. I have never felt so afraid, alone, or unsure about anything.

Finally, I worked out a thought in my mind. I had been happy before joining the Church, and now I was miserable! I called Brother Kocherhans, the man who had taught and baptized me. He agreed to meet me at the chapel that evening. As we sat in a small, cold classroom, I wept as I tried to explain all that had been happening to me. After laying out all my arguments for why I never should have joined Brother Kocherhans's church, I concluded by saying, "I used to be happy. If your church is so right, why have I been so miserable since I joined?"

Brother Kocherhans was quick to correct my idea that it was *his* church I had joined. "The Church of Jesus Christ of Latter-day Saints is the Lord's Church," he quietly taught. Then looking at me with piercing eyes, he asked a question I've never forgotten: "What are you *not* doing that prevents you from having the Holy Ghost as your companion?"

This was too much! I responded in disgust, "I'm not doing anything!"

"Are you reading the scriptures every day? Are you praying daily?" he asked.

"No!" I responded in anger. I didn't bother to explain that in my confusion and frustration, these were the *last* things I even thought about doing. I was barely keeping my head above water!

"Carolyn," Brother Kocherhans said in a stern but kindly manner, "I want you to go home now. As soon as you arrive home, go to your room and kneel in prayer. Thank Heavenly Father for His many blessings to you, talk with Him about how you are feeling, and ask for His help. Then read one chapter in the Book of Mormon. Do these things every day. We'll talk again."

I left without making a commitment, but because of my great respect for Brother Kocherhans, I followed his counsel and began that very evening. No miracles occurred, no angels appeared, no confirmation that what I had done was apparent to me. But over the weeks, the turmoil and confusion I had experienced were replaced with feelings of peace and faith—two of the fruits of the Spirit identified by Paul in his epistle to the Galatians (see Galatians 5:22–23).

Several weeks after I returned to daily scripture study and prayer, Sister Kocherhans called to ask if I could help her with something.

"Oh, sure, what can I do?"

"Do you have the book *Jesus the Christ*?" she asked.

When I told her I did, she asked if I would get it while she was still on the phone. Asking me to turn to a specific page, she invited me to come to Relief Society and help her with the Spiritual Living lesson by discussing my understanding of what Elder Talmage had written. I did so and felt the embracing love and acceptance of the sisters in the ward.

I believe that Brother and Sister Kocherhans taught me the basic elements of how to *fortify* myself spiritually. I know of no list entitled, "Things to Do to Fortify Ourselves Spiritually."

If I were to create such a list, however, I would include prayer and scripture study at the very top. The list would also include things such as temple worship, giving service, fasting, obedience, partaking of the sacrament, and much more.

Years ago I was in the Philippines on a Church assignment to teach leadership skills to young women. I asked them questions and tried to involve them in role-playing activities, but because they were more used to speaking Tagalog than English, I could not understand them, and I wondered if they could understand me. After the first day of teaching I felt discouraged. I prayed that night that we would be able to understand each other as I taught in the various locations throughout the Philippine islands.

From that day on, I could understand the young women, and their nodding heads and laughter helped me to know that they understood me as well. No wonder Alma taught his son Helaman, "Cry unto God for all thy support. . . . Counsel with the Lord in all thy doings, and he will direct thee for good; yea, when thou liest down at night lie down unto the Lord, that he may watch over you in your sleep; and when thou risest in the morning let thy heart be full of thanks unto God" (Alma 37:36–37).

Studying the words of the Lord recorded in the scriptures is another way of our communicating with Him—and of His communicating with us. To be honest, I have a love affair with the scriptures, just as President Gordon B. Hinckley promised: "I hope that for you this [emphasis on reading the scriptures] will become something far more enjoyable than a duty; that, rather, it will become a love affair with the word of God."[8]

One of the keys to the power of scripture study is in 1 Nephi 1—on page 2 of the Book of Mormon. You will remember that Father Lehi was overcome with the Spirit and was carried away in a vision. In addition to seeing God and numberless concourses of angels, he saw One and twelve others following Him. The first stood before Lehi, "gave unto him a book, and bade him that he should read." We are pretty safe in assuming that this was a book of scripture of some kind because it was delivered by the Son of God. Then follows the key, one of the reasons for which we read the scriptures: "And it came to pass that as he read, he was filled with the Spirit of the Lord" (1 Nephi 1:11–12; see also vv. 7–10).

President Brigham Young told of a sacred experience when the martyred Prophet Joseph Smith came to him in a vision. President Young asked if he had a message for the people. The Prophet said: "Tell the people to be humble and faithful, and be sure to keep the spirit of the Lord and it will lead them aright. Be careful and not turn away the still small voice; it will teach you what to do and where to go."[9]

Can you think of any more timely message for us as we seek to *fortify* ourselves against the temptations, busyness, and pressures of our day? Remember Lehi's experience—"as he read, he was filled with the Spirit of the Lord." Reading the scriptures is a way to fortify ourselves because it puts us in tune with the Spirit of the Lord.

Elder Dallin H. Oaks clearly stated the relationship of scripture study to personal revelation:

> SCRIPTURE READING PUTS US
>
> IN TUNE WITH THE SPIRIT
>
> OF THE LORD.
>
> *Elder Dallin H. Oaks*

"Just as continuing revelation enlarges and illuminates the scriptures, so also a study of the scriptures enables men and women to receive revelations. . . . This happens because scripture reading puts us in tune with the Spirit of the Lord.

"The idea that scripture reading can lead to inspiration and revelation opens the door to the truth that a scripture is not limited to what it meant when it was written but may also include what that scripture means to a reader today. Even more, scripture reading may also lead to current revelation on whatever else the Lord wishes to communicate to the reader at that time. We do not overstate the point when we say that the scriptures can be a Urim and Thummim to assist each of us to receive personal revelation.

"Because we believe that scripture reading can help us receive revelation, we are encouraged to read the scriptures again and again. By this means, we obtain access to what our Heavenly Father would have us know and do in our personal lives today. That is one reason Latter-day Saints believe in *daily* scripture study."[10]

Elder Bruce R. McConkie said, "I sometimes think that one of the best-kept secrets of the kingdom is that the scriptures open the door to the receipt of revelation."[11]

At the time we are confirmed members of The Church of Jesus Christ of Latter-day Saints, we are given a gift that can fortify us throughout our lives. We are invited to "receive the Holy Ghost." I believe this invitation means much more than the initial receipt of this precious gift. It is in fact an invitation to receive this gift every day of our lives. If we are consciously trying to live as guided by the Spirit and to learn to hear the voice of the Lord, we will be fortified against any negative or evil influence in the world. Is it any wonder that the Nephites, who were taught and tutored by the Savior following His resurrection, "pray[ed] for that which they most desired; and they desired that the Holy Ghost should be given unto them"?

(3 Nephi 19:9). They knew the Savior would soon leave their presence, but they also knew that "by the power of the Holy Ghost [they could] know the truth of all things" (Moroni 10:5).

I am sure there are challenges you face in your life, things that are in your heart about which you can speak to no one except a loving Heavenly Father, who knows and loves you. I do not know what kinds of difficulties each of us, individually or collectively, will face in the future. But I do know that *now* is the time to *fortify* ourselves. As we listen to the living prophets, we sense that *spiritual fortification* is critical. If we heed their counsel, we will be like those whom Moroni prepared against the attack of the enemy—strong, secure, and powerful (see Alma 49). Then, like the people of Nephi, we will "thank the Lord . . . because of his matchless power in delivering [us] from the hands of [our] enemies" (Alma 49:28).

GETTING STARTED

1. Study the conference talks in the *Ensign* or *Liahona.* A useful exercise is to identify *warnings, promises,* and *counsel* given by our living prophets. You might want to mark each of the categories in a different color ink. Often, you will find repetition in many of the messages. Rather than thinking, "We never hear anything new at conference," we may learn from

the teaching of Elder Henry B. Eyring: "When the words of prophets seem repetitive, that should rivet our attention."[12]

2. Read Alma 49–50. Look for the following words and phrases: "fortifying," "assurance of protection," "strongholds," "forts of security," and "places of security." Ponder what you might do to apply these words and phrases to your personal life, the life of your family, and your home.

3. If you desire to begin a regular scripture study program, consider purchasing *Preach My Gospel,* the guidebook for missionaries. Study the referenced scriptures and learn the doctrines and principles they teach.

4. Another way you might study the scriptures is to read the *Ensign* or *Liahona* and mark scriptures that have particular meaning to you. If you use a conference issue, you might choose to mark scriptures used by the general authorities and general officers of the Church.

5. Read and ponder the Bible Dictionary definition of *prayer.*[13]

Scriptures and Thoughts to Ponder

Elder Spencer W. Kimball: "I find that when I get casual in my relationships with divinity and when it seems that no divine ear is listening and no divine voice is speaking, that I am far, far away. If I immerse myself in the scriptures the distance narrows and spirituality returns."[14]

"And now, as the preaching of the word had a great tendency to lead the people to do that which was just—yea, it had had more powerful effect upon the minds of the people than the sword, or anything else, which had happened unto them— therefore Alma thought it was expedient that they should try the virtue of the word of God" (Alma 31:5; see also Alma 4:18–19; Helaman 5:4).

Elder W. Don Ladd: "We all need to build a personal ark, to fortify ourselves against this rising tide of evil, to protect ourselves and our families against the floodwaters of iniquity around us. And we shouldn't wait until it starts raining, but prepare in advance."[15]

President Ezra Taft Benson: "May I admonish you to participate in a program of daily reading and pondering of the scriptures. . . . The Book of Mormon will change your life. It will

fortify you against the evils of our day. It will bring a spirituality into your life that no other book will."[16]

Kathleen H. Hughes: "Scripture study and prayer will bring
change—but not automatically. If we read with one eye and
pray with half a heart, we are engaging in a ritual, and while
that time is not worthless, it isn't fully productive either. We
need, with the support of family, to clear enough time to
study—not just read—to contemplate, feel, and wait for
answers. The Lord has promised that He will strengthen us,
fortify and refresh us, if we will take time for Him each day
(see D&C 88:63)."[17]

The power is in them,
wherein they are agents
unto themselves.

—Doctrine and Covenants 58:28

you

nine

Dear Friend,

As we come to the end of our conversation together through these pages, my thoughts are *of you* and *for you.* Writing this book has been an exciting and lengthy learning process for me. Quite frankly, this book evolved from my own need to simplify my life. While I was serving a full-time mission, life had seemed so focused, so unburdened, and so simple. There were few distractions when my companion and I were at our flat—rarely a phone call, no junk mail, and no television or radio. The kitchen was adequate, and getting along with only four forks and knives proved no problem. In fact, two pots and a skillet filled all our needs. I soon discovered that even the minimal list of clothing suggested by the Missionary Department was more than I needed, and I shipped a box of clothing back to my home. As I anticipated my release, I began to think of the life I had left prior to my mission—a busy, often out-of-control and stressful life. I was determined to live the simple life of a missionary when I got home.

Within a few hours after I arrived home, however, the phone began to ring incessantly. I found myself startled each time I heard the loud "ring—ring." The day I was released, a friend who had been my accountant and bill-payer for eighteen months presented me with a large box containing receipts, papers, documents, reports, and stacks of Christmas cards received two months prior. Some things needed immediate attention. My sister-in-law from Ohio called to tell me she was just completing a ski vacation in Utah and asked me to meet her at the airport that afternoon. Although I'd been invited to a friend's home for dinner, I decided to squeeze in the visit at the airport.

The next day the mail arrived. There were bills to pay and junk mail I hadn't asked for and didn't want. Many pieces required shredding because my name, address, and other personal information were on them. Boxes I had sent from New Zealand began arriving, and I wondered why I had mailed more things home.

I came to an immediate discovery—the simple life and

schedule of a missionary was impossible! I'd been relieved of many necessary duties for eighteen months, but living "in the world" requires attention to many details and people and obligations.

It was then, more than two years ago, that I began thinking of how I could simplify my life in this busy world in which we live. I read books about how to simplify life, but I was soon disillusioned, as many focused on getting rid of clutter, organizing a grocery list, eliminating call waiting, and living with fewer clothes. Although I found some of the suggestions helpful, I felt that the books I read missed the mark—at least for me.

I apologize if you expected a lot of how-to's—how to clean the refrigerator with ease, organize closets efficiently once and for all, avoid hectic schedules, and eliminate unwanted interruptions. I thought at first that this book would include such things. But the longer I lived with *simplify,* the more convinced I became that simplification has much more to do with the spiritual aspect of our lives than with temporal things.

I still remember the day I was reading the Doctrine and Covenants and stumbled onto the scripture from section 101:37: "Care for . . . the life of the soul." I was elated! It confirmed what I had been thinking. Several weeks later, I came across a talk by Elder Neal A. Maxwell entitled "Care for the Life of the Soul."[1]

Gradually I came to understand that simplifying is about enhancing our ability to focus on things that *really* matter, to deliberately choose our priorities, and to refuse to let unimportant things take over the things of real importance.

My greatest fear is that you might feel overwhelmed or inadequate as you ponder my personal experiences or ideas. Please don't think that my intention is to pile on more things that you have to do. Everything in this book comes with only one instruction: *Use as needed.*

I struggled to know if adding a "Getting Started" section at the end of each chapter would be helpful or if it would only be a reminder of something else you felt you had to do. The suggestions there, as well as the section called "Scriptures and Thoughts to Ponder," are only meant to help—*never* to cause feelings of guilt or added stress.

My hope is that as you have read this book there were times when the impressions of the Holy Ghost came into your heart or mind, times when you felt "I could do that, and my life would be calmer, more peaceful, and simpler." I hope that you paid much more attention to those promptings than to anything you read here, because the Spirit is the member of the Godhead who will help you "know the truth of all things" (Moroni 10:5).

Please know, too, that learning to simplify has been a process for me. It will continue to be for the rest of my life. Circumstances, responsibilities, health, Church callings, living conditions—all these things change, and so do we. I also wish I could report that since writing this book I never feel stressed, overwhelmed, or out of control. The truth is, I still battle such feelings—though I do think I'm improving.

Now it is time for you to determine what action you will take. You may lay the book aside and never look at it again—no one will know. You can choose to let an idea or a thought prompted by the Holy Ghost guide something you want to change—to start doing or to stop doing—that will help you simplify your life.

Now that you've read through the book, review the guidelines suggested in the Introduction. You might see them in a very different way.

1. What appears simple is usually not easy.

2. There are many right ways to do things. In fact, there may be no right or wrong way to simplify your life. Yours is an individual quest.

3. Changing attitudes and ways of doing takes time. Do not create self-imposed deadlines.

4. It is impossible to add something to your life without taking something away. There are only twenty-four hours in a day, and most people in our society are already sleep deprived.

5. Introspection is critical to transformation.

6. Although many external conditions are beyond our control, we are always capable of making internal decisions.

7. Change is *always* possible. One of the most important things you can do is to ask our Heavenly Father, in prayer, what you need to change and what steps you need to take to bring about this change.

8. This book is not for speed-reading. Choose a chapter, thought, or idea that has interest or meaning to you, think about it, and be sensitive to the promptings of the Holy Ghost. Too often we ignore thoughts and feelings that come to us when we read or hear an idea. Remember the Savior's counsel: "Behold, I will tell you in your mind [thoughts] and in your heart [feelings], by the Holy Ghost. . . . this is the spirit of revelation" (D&C 8:2–3).

There are many things I want to change in my life— things that will help me to draw closer to the Savior, to be more in tune with the Spirit, to fortify myself spiritually for the future. I know I can't do everything all at once. Just like you, I pray to choose carefully.

I am humbled as I review what I've written. I bear

testimony that many of the ideas presented in this book came from promptings I received from the Holy Ghost. I know of the power of Christ's grace in my life, of His power to strengthen us beyond our natural abilities. I pray that you, too, will feel of His power in your life as you accept the challenge to simplify your life and care for the life of your soul. I bear testimony that divine help and strength is available to each of us, in the name of Jesus Christ, amen.

Love,
Carolyn

chapter one
introduction

1. Kapp, *Joy of the Journey,* 4–5.
2. See Ballard, "O Be Wise," 17.

chapter two
stillness

1. Lindbergh, *Gift from the Sea,* 27.
2. Ibid., 40.
3. Hinckley, "Each a Better Person," 100.
4. Packer, BYU–Hawaii Commencement Address, December 17, 2005.
5. *Webster's New World Dictionary,* s.v. "commune."
6. Lorin F. Wheelwright, "Oh, May My Soul Commune with Thee," in *Hymns,* no. 123; used by permission.
7. Pearce, *Heart like His,* 90.

8. Naomi W. Randall, "When Faith Endures," in *Hymns,* no. 128.

9. Hinckley, *Teachings of Gordon B. Hinckley,* 608–9.

10. Perry, "When I Feel His Love"; used by permission.

11. Faust, "Standing in Holy Places," 62.

12. *David O. McKay,* 31–32.

13. Rasmus, "I Feel at Peace," 10–11.

chapter three
integrity

1. John Young; notes in possession of author.

2. Bennett, *Book of Virtues,* 657.

3. Toufexis, "Shape of the Nation."

4. McCabe, www.academicintegrity.org/cai_research.asp.

5. Hinckley, "Shepherds of the Flock," 51; emphasis added

6. Faust, "Honesty—a Moral Compass," 42; emphasis in original.

7. Whitney, *Life of Heber C. Kimball,* 446.

8. Hinckley, *Be Thou An Example,* 27, 28; emphasis added.

9. Maeser, in *Vital Quotations,* 167.

10. Humes, *Wit and Wisdom of Abraham Lincoln,* 9–10.

11. Kimball, *BYU Speeches,* February 25, 1964, 2–3.

12. Hinckley, *Teachings of Gordon B. Hinckley,* 265–66.

13. Jeb McGruder, as quoted in "Boy Scout without a Compass," *Time,* June 3, 1974.

14. William Shakespeare, *Antony and Cleopatra,* 3.4.24–25.

chapter four
mercy

1. Monson, "Mercy—The Divine Gift," 59.

2. Hinckley, "Blessed Are the Merciful," 68; emphasis added.

3. Webster, *American Dictionary of the English Language,* s.v. "mercy."
4. Hinckley, "Blessed Are the Merciful," 69.
5. Oaks, *With Full Purpose of Heart,* 116.
6. Ibid., 117.
7. Used by permission; name withheld.
8. Packer, "Brilliant Morning of Forgiveness," 19; emphasis altered.
9. Smith, *Teachings of the Prophet Joseph Smith,* 191; emphasis added.
10. LDS Bible Dictionary, s.v. "repentance," 760.
11. See Clark, "God Hath Prepared a More Excellent Way."
12. Holland, "Come unto Me," 19.
13. William Shakespeare, *Merchant of Venice,* 4.1.184–95.
14. Hinckley, "Blessed Are the Merciful," 70.
15. Packer, "Brilliant Morning of Forgiveness," 20.
16. Julius Schubring, "Cast Thy Burden upon the Lord," in *Hymns,* no. 110.
17. Hanks, "My Specialty Is Mercy," 75.

chapter five
prune

1. Brown, "Currant Bush," 12–14.
2. *Roget's New Millennium Thesaurus, First Edition* (v 1.3.1), from Thesaurus.com. Accessed December 2006.
3. Oaks, "Focus and Priorities," 82; emphasis added.
4. Scott, "First Things First," 9.
5. LDS Bible Dictionary, s.v. "repentance," 760.
6. Ballard, "Be Strong in the Lord," 13.
7. Oaks, "Focus and Priorities," 82, 83, 84.
8. Ballard, "Keeping Life's Demands in Balance," 14.
9. Wirthlin, "Follow Me," 16.

10. Bradford, "Selfless Service," 76.
11. Holland, "'One Thing Needful': Becoming Women of Greater Faith in Christ," 26; emphasis in original; used by permission.
12. *New Era*, August 2006, 17.
13. Scott, "First Things First," 7.

chapter six
let go

1. Webster, *American Dictionary of the English Language,* s.v. "cumber."
2. Maxwell, "Care for the Life of the Soul," 68.
3. "He Offended Me!" 17–19.
4. Packer, "Balm of Gilead," 16–18; emphasis added; used by permission.
5. "There Is a Balm in Gilead," traditional African-American spiritual, from www.negrospirituals.com. Accessed December 2006.
6. Cannon, *Gospel Truth,* 3; emphasis added.
7. Packer, "Little Children," 17.
8. Christensen, "My Personal Parable for Peace," 9.
9. Packer, "Balm of Gilead," 18.
10. Wirthlin, "Follow Me," 16.
11. Peterson, "Exhaustion Is Not a Prerequisite to Perfection," 52.

chapter seven
impossible

1. Maxwell, "Take Especial Care of Your Family," 89.
2. Scott, "Doctrinal Foundation of the Auxiliaries," 67.
3. LDS Bible Dictionary, s.v. "grace," 697.
4. Bednar, "In the Strength of the Lord."

5. Personal interview with author, February 27, 2006.

6. Personal correspondence with author, March 28, 2006.

7. Personal interview with author, February 22, 2006.

8. Holland, "Come unto Me," 19.

9. Theodore E. Curtis, "Lean on My Ample Arm," in *Hymns,* no. 120.

10. Attributed to Robert Keen, "How Firm a Foundation," in *Hymns,* no. 85.

11. LDS Bible Dictionary, s.v. "grace," 697; emphasis added.

12. William Clayton, "Come, Come, Ye Saints," in *Hymns,* no. 30.

13. *True to the Faith,* 78.

14. Joseph L. Townsend, "Reverently and Meekly Now," in *Hymns,* no. 185.

15. Maxwell, "Plow in Hope," 60.

16. Barney, "No Toil nor Labor Fear," 37.

chapter eight
fortify

1. Martin Luther, "A Mighty Fortress Is Our God," in *Hymns,* no. 68; emphasis added.

2. *Random House Dictionary,* s.v. "fortify."

3. Bradford, "Selfless Service," 75.

4. Hinckley, "Standing Strong and Immovable," 20.

5. Packer, "On the Shoulders of Giants," 7.

6. Oaks, "Preparation for the Second Coming," 9.

7. Eyring, "Always," 9, 12.

8. Hinckley, *Teachings of Gordon B. Hinckley,* 573–74.

9. Watson, *Manuscript History of Brigham Young,* February 23, 1847.

10. Oaks, "Scripture Reading and Revelation," 7; emphasis in original.

11. McConkie, *Doctrines of the Restoration,* 243.

12. Eyring, "Finding Safety in Counsel," 25.

13. LDS Bible Dictionary, s.v. "prayer," 752–53.

14. Kimball, *Teachings of Spencer W. Kimball,* 135.

15. Ladd, "Make Thee an Ark," 29.

16. Benson, "To the 'Youth of the Noble Birthright,'" 43.

17. Hughes, "Out of Small Things," 109.

chapter nine

you

1. Maxwell, "Care for the Life of the Soul," 68–70.

sources

Anonymous. "He Offended Me!" *Ensign,* January 2006.

Ballard, M. Russell. "Be Strong in the Lord." *Ensign,* July 2004.

———. "Keeping Life's Demands in Balance." *Ensign,* May 1987.

———. "O Be Wise." *Ensign,* November 2006.

Barney, Ronald O. " 'No Toil nor Labor Fear.'" *Ensign,* February 1997.

Bednar, David A. "In the Strength of the Lord." BYU–Idaho Devotional, January 8, 2002.

Bennett, William. *The Book of Virtues.* New York: Simon and Schuster, 1993.

Benson, Ezra Taft. "To the 'Youth of the Noble Birthright.'" *Ensign,* May 1986.

"Boy Scout without a Compass." *Time,* June 3, 1974.

Bradford, William R. "Selfless Service," *Ensign,* November 1987.

Brown, Hugh B. "The Currant Bush." *New Era,* April 2001.

Cannon, George Q. *Gospel Truth.* Salt Lake City: Deseret Book, 1987.

Christensen, Nancy M. "My Personal Parable for Peace." *Ensign,* July 2006.

Clark, Kim B. "God Hath Prepared a More Excellent Way." BYU–Idaho Devotional, September 5, 2006.

Eyring, Henry B. "Always." *Ensign,* October 1999.

———. "Finding Safety in Counsel." *Ensign,* May 1997.

Faust, James E. "Honesty—a Moral Compass." *Ensign,* November 1996.

———. "Standing in Holy Places." *Ensign,* May 2005.

"He Offended Me!" *Ensign,* January 2006.

Hanks, Marion D. "My Specialty Is Mercy." *Ensign,* November 1981.

Hinckley, Gordon B. *Be Thou an Example.* Salt Lake City: Deseret Book, 1981.

———. "Blessed Are the Merciful." *Ensign,* May 1990.

———. "Each a Better Person." *Ensign,* November 2002.

———. "The Shepherds of the Flock." *Ensign,* May 1999.

———. "Standing Strong and Immovable." Worldwide Leadership Training Meeting, January 10, 2004, 20.

———. *Teachings of Gordon B. Hinckley.* Salt Lake City: Deseret Book, 1997.

Holland, Jeffrey R. "Come unto Me." *Ensign,* April 1998.

Holland, Patricia T. "'One Thing Needful': Becoming Women of Greater Faith in Christ." *Ensign,* October 1987.

Hughes, Kathleen H. "Out of Small Things." *Ensign,* November 2004.

Humes, James C., ed. *The Wit and Wisdom of Abraham Lincoln.* New York: Gramercy, 1996.

Hymns of The Church of Jesus Christ of Latter-day Saints. Salt Lake City: The Church of Jesus Christ of Latter-day Saints, 1985.

Kapp, Ardeth G. *The Joy of the Journey.* Salt Lake City: Deseret Book, 1992.

Kimball, Spencer W. *BYU Speeches of the Year.* Provo, Brigham Young University, February 25, 1964.

————. *Teachings of Spencer W. Kimball.* Edited by Edward L. Kimball. Salt Lake City: Deseret Book, 2002.

Ladd, W. Don. "Make Thee an Ark." *Ensign,* November 1994.

Lindbergh, Anne Morrow. *Gift from the Sea.* Toronto: Random House, 1992.

Maeser, Karl G. In *Vital Quotations.* Compiled by Emerson Roy West. Salt Lake City: Bookcraft, 1968.

Maxwell, Neal A. "Care for the Life of the Soul." *Ensign,* May 2003.

————. "Plow in Hope." *Ensign,* May 2001.

————. "Take Especial Care of Your Family." *Ensign,* May 1994.

McCabe, Don. www.academicintegrity.org/cai_research.asp. Accessed November 2006.

McConkie, Bruce R. *Doctrines of the Restoration.* Edited by Mark L. McConkie. Salt Lake City: Bookcraft, 1989.

McKay, David O. *David O. McKay.* A volume in *Teachings of Presidents of the Church* series. Salt Lake City: The Church of Jesus Christ of Latter-day Saints, 2003.

Monson, Thomas S. "Mercy—The Divine Gift." *Ensign,* May 1995.

New Era. August 2006.

Oaks, Dallin H. "Focus and Priorities." *Ensign,* May 2001.

————. "Preparation for the Second Coming." *Ensign,* May 2004.

————. "Scripture Reading and Revelation." *Ensign,* January 1995.

————. *With Full Purpose of Heart.* Salt Lake City: Deseret Book, 2002.

Packer, Boyd K. "Balm of Gilead." *Ensign,* November 1987.

————. "The Brilliant Morning of Forgiveness." *Ensign,* November 1995.

————. BYU–Hawaii Commencement Address. Laie, Hawaii, December 17, 2005.

————. "Little Children." *Ensign,* November 1986.

————. "On the Shoulders of Giants." Address delivered at J. Reuben

Clark Law Society, Brigham Young University, Provo, Utah, February 28, 2004.

Pearce, Virginia H. *A Heart like His.* Salt Lake City: Deseret Book, 2006.

Perry, Janice Kapp. "When I Feel His Love." Written for the Relief Society General Meeting, September 2005.

Peterson, Cindy K. "Exhaustion Is Not a Prerequisite to Perfection." *Ensign,* October 1993.

Rasmus, Carolyn J. "I Feel at Peace." *New Era,* February 1993.

Scott, Richard G. "The Doctrinal Foundation of the Auxiliaries." *Ensign,* August 2005.

———. "First Things First." *Ensign,* May 2001.

Smith, Joseph. *Teachings of the Prophet Joseph Smith.* Selected by Joseph Fielding Smith. Salt Lake City: Deseret Book, 1976.

"There Is a Balm in Gilead." Traditional African-American spiritual. Accessed at www.negrospirituals.com December 2006.

Toufexis, Anastasia. "The Shape of the Nation." *Time,* October 7, 1985.

True to the Faith: A Gospel Reference. Salt Lake City: The Church of Jesus Christ of Latter-day Saints, 2004.

Watson, Eldon J. *Manuscript History of Brigham Young, 1846–1847.* Salt Lake City: E. J. Watson, 1971.

Webster, Noah. *American Dictionary of the English Language.* 1828. Reprint, San Francisco: Foundation for American Christian Education, 1980.

Whitney, Orson F. *Life of Heber C. Kimball.* Salt Lake City: Bookcraft, 1945.

Wirthlin, Joseph B. "Follow Me." *Ensign,* May 2002.

Young, Brigham. Manuscript History of Brigham Young 1846–1847, February 23, 1847. Salt Lake City, Archives of The Church of Jesus Christ of Latter-day Saints.

index